T0361893

Rethinking the Enterprise
Competitiveness, Technology and Society
Restoring the ethical and political dimension to economic action

RETHINKING the ENTERPRISE

COMPETITIVENESS, TECHNOLOGY AND SOCIETY
Restoring the ethical and political dimension to economic action

Philippe de Woot

Greenleaf
PUBLISHING

Published by
Greenleaf Publishing Limited
Aizlewood's Mill, Nursery Street
Sheffield S3 8GG, UK
www.greenleaf-publishing.com

original edition *Repenser L'entreprise*
Ed. L' Académie en poche
Académie Royale des Sciences, des Lettres et des Beaux-arts de Belgique

Cover concept by Jebens Design for EFMD's *Global Focus* magazine

MIX
Paper from
responsible sources
FSC
www.fsc.org   FSC® C013604

Printed in the United Kingdom
Printed and bound by CPI Group (UK) Ltd, Croydon, CR0 4YY

British Library Cataloguing in Publication Data:
 A catalogue record for this book is available from the British Library.
  ISBN-13: 9781783531462 [paperback]
  ISBN-13: 9781783532261 [hardback]
  ISBN-13: 9781783531486 [PDF ebook]
  ISBN-13: 9781783531479 [ePub ebook]

Prometheus: I brought them the treasures of the earth:
I brought them gold and silver, bronze and iron,
I brought them industry and art
I took from man expectancy of death.

Oceanus: What medicine found'st thou for this malady?

Prometheus: I planted blind hope in the heart of him.

(Aeschylus)

Man is obviously made to think. Therein lies all his dignity and
    his merit
. . . Now of what does the world think? . . . of running at the ring
        . . . fighting . . . making oneself king,
Without thinking what it is to be a king and what to be a man

(Pascal)

The sleep of reason brings forth monsters.

(Goya)

Contents

Author's note

This essay, while following their conceptual approach, seeks to enrich certain theses of the books I published in 2005 and 2009[1]: an evolution of the system is possible, but it requires a more radical approach than that outlined a few years ago. It is only by changing its culture in depth that enterprise can restore the ethical and political dimension to its acts.

1 P. de Woot, *La responsabilité sociale des entreprises: Faut-il enchaîner Prométhée?* (Economica, 2005); and *Should Prometheus Be Bound? Corporate Global Responsibility* (Palgrave Macmillan, 2005, 2009).

P. de Woot, *Lettre ouverte aux dirigeants chrétiens en temps d'urgence* (Desclée de Brouwer, 2009).

P. de Woot, *Spirituality and Business. A Christian Viewpoint* (GSE Research Ltd, 2013).

Introduction

If there is a key trend in our time, it is that of the progress of science and technology. This trend has become a steamroller, whatever the vagaries of history and economic conditions. Science has undergone an unprecedented acceleration in the last century, and several factors have contributed to this: the very accumulation of knowledge and its rapid dissemination have provided researchers with broader and more ambitious research fields, with inter-disciplinary approaches and universal access to information fostering new and bolder research. Technological competition, now global, has expanded and multiplied the means of funding research and development. We have got to the heart of many secrets that seemed indecipherable just a few decades ago. We have discovered the mechanisms of life. We have come up with precise figures on the origin of the universe; we have discovered its first moments and are beginning to know 'the music of the stars'.

It is enterprise that transforms, often as soon as they emerge, scientific knowledge and technologies into products and services. By mastering the methods and tools of techno-science, it has the power of knowledge behind its economic strategies. Techno-science constantly provides new opportunities and more powerful competitive weapons. It thus becomes a key element of economic development and competitive power. Enterprise is therefore the main mediator between science and society. Yet is it an agent of progress? This is the question that this essay proposes to discuss.

Questioning the purpose of enterprise and the development model that drives it means questioning material progress, its orientation and its ambiguities. This question has intrigued humans since the beginning of civilisation. Greek myths extensively discussed it, and place it in its proper perspective, which is that of creative impulse, but also the concerns of men. For them, the creators of material progress played a major role in society. They were heroes, but damned heroes. Everything happens as if technical progress since the dawn of time was perceived as beneficial and dangerous at the same time, as essentially ambiguous. Their approach leads to the question of whether men, these 'ephemeral beings', can appropriate mastery of technology without finalising it, or subjecting it to a broader vision of the common good. A question which, in various ways, transcends history.

Enterprise being the ultimate agent of economic and technical creativity, it was long believed that its acts automatically served the common good through the virtues of the market and its famous 'invisible hand'. Undoubtedly, the market economy has been a source of considerable progress for part of humanity that it lifted out of poverty. Many leaders justify this system by saying that, overall, the benefits outweigh the disadvantages.

Today, the link between economic growth and the common good has become less clear. A globalised, neoliberal approach has gradually 'delinked' economics from ethics and politics.

Globalisation, the acceleration of techno-science and the lack of global regulation give the economic system autonomy and unprecedented power. It operates according to its own criteria: profitability, competitiveness, the race to win market share. In the absence of global regulation, this approach tends to become dominant, and imposes a development model upon us that has no purpose other than its effectiveness and dynamism. Led solely by its own instrumental logic, this model becomes increasingly ambiguous and paradoxical. While providing economic growth unprecedented in human history, our model runs out of control, pollutes, excludes and generates phenomena of domination, injustice and social disintegration. Never has our ability to create wealth been greater, and never has the absolute number of people in poverty been so high; never has our scientific and technical knowledge been so great, and never has the planet been so threatened; never has the need for economic governance been so compelling, and never have governments of nation-states been so toothless.

This raises the question of whether the current model is still politically and morally acceptable without a profound change. One might even ask if we are not completely blinded to the excesses of it, if we are not complicit in its overall malfunctions, and if they do not lead us into a kind of madness. Our model generates systemic risks which are not explicitly desired and are difficult to measure, albeit not unexpected, and whose consequences can endanger social harmony, existing regulations and institutions and the planet itself. We are in a high-risk society that forces us to question ourselves, to take more responsibility, to invent new modes of cooperation and governance.

The challenges of the 21st century are immense: implementing a more sustainable development model, maintaining markets and societies to be as open as possible, deploying entrepreneurial dynamism in the service of the common good, boosting employment, reindustrialising Western countries while promoting the development of emerging countries . . . How can we better focus our extraordinary creative capacity to meet the challenges ahead?

Enterprise is the central agent of the economic system. This essay therefore will focus on it, not to impute full responsibility for the excesses and failures of our economic model, but rather to outline the role it could play in its transformation. By changing its culture, it can be a powerful tool to better meet the global challenges of our century. Given the power it holds over resources, enterprise therefore has a major responsibility.

A central theme of this essay is that a spirit of enterprise, creativity and innovation are necessary responses to societal challenges. Although the current economic model is the source of major deviations, enterprise in the broadest sense can help correct many of them. From *problem* it can become *solution*. This approach is particularly realistic today given that creativity, innovation and entrepreneurial activity go far beyond the scope of capitalist enterprise and market. Thousands of initiatives appear throughout the world to propose solutions: social entrepreneurship, the social economy, fair trade . . . They are a sign of devolved and more accountable entrepreneurial activities. Many of them cooperate with capitalist enterprises that are inspired to transform their culture and meet their social responsibilities. This abundance of creativity brings with it new forms of enterprise which, far from competing with more conventional forms, are an indispensable complement and a source of cultural inspiration.

Many companies, among the most enlightened, have already begun this process. But alone they are not enough to restore the ethical and political dimensions to economic activity. Enterprise is obviously one stakeholder among others. The public authorities, social forces and civil society are expected to contribute to this transformation.

1

Drifts and deviations of the market economy

1.1 A high-performing model

Our business model is that of a **competitive market economy**. To various extents, it is today imposed across almost the entire planet. This model has shown its effectiveness and its ability to create wealth and has led to economic growth unprecedented in human history. Built on free enterprise, free trade and competition, it is dynamic and creative in essence.

The **market** organises trade. It is an achievement of civilisation. It advantageously replaces theft, looting and raiding. Trade is a source of contacts, openness and freedom. From its outset, trade has been considered as a driver of economic development, it is true, but also as a way of supporting the reconciliation of peoples and cultural developments. As Frederick Tristan put it so well, 'The Venetians are traders, but what genius does it take to turn salt and dried fish into silks and spices, and these into Giorgione and Palladio!'[1]

Competition—running together—tends to see the best enterprise win and gives the consumer a constant improvement in the quality/price ratio. Even if it does not work perfectly, competition powers the system and gives it its dynamism and creativity. Remember that **innovation** is at the heart of effective competition and that it is technology which in the long run provides it with the decisive weapons. Schumpeter showed the real competition was that which replaced the old with the new, which killed off the existing product to replace it with a product that hitherto did not exist: it is the famous **creative destruction**.

For Schumpeter, economic development depends on **innovation**, the agent of which is an extraordinary personality: the **entrepreneur**. He has some very

---

1 F. Tristan, *Venise* (Paris: Editions du Champ Vallon, diffusion PUF, 1984).

specific qualities: the **vision** of possible progress, energy and a sufficient taste for **risk** to implement it, and a **power of conviction** that can bring about the necessary support and resources. The innovative entrepreneur, through his or her very creativity, transforms the nature of competition. Instead of being limited to a simple price war, it becomes a race towards innovation and technological progress.

> The competition that really matters is competition from new goods, new techniques, new sources, new types of organisation (control of larger units, for example), competition which commands a decisive cost advantage or quality, and which impacts not on the profit margins and quantities produced by existing firms, but their foundations and their very existence. This form of competition is much more effective than the other, in the same way as a bombardment is more effective than merely forcing a door. It is so much more important that it becomes relatively indifferent whether competition in the ordinary sense functions more or less effectively; the powerful lever that in the long run increases production and lowers prices is, anyway, exerted in a different way. The problem usually considered is to establish how capitalism administers existing structures, whereas the

important issue is to discover how it creates and destroys structures.[2]

As the Louvain school has shown[3] and, more recently, the American economist Baumol,[4] it is not only the individual entrepreneur who creates innovation. Enterprise itself has taken on much of this role and now provides economic creativity in a collective and systematic manner. To survive in the long term, enterprise has become a **collective entrepreneur**. The reality of economic and technological development is one of major innovations often implemented at first by individual entrepreneurs, rapidly passed on by public entrepreneurs that are corporations. Today, the names of Ford, Campbell, Solvay, Bekaert, Lafarge,

2 J. Schumpeter, *The Theory of Economic Development* (Harvard University Press, 1949).

3 L. Dupriez, *Des mouvements économiques généraux* (Louvain, Belgium: Nauwelaerts, 1949); *Philosophie des conjonctures économiques* (Louvain, Belgium: Nauwelaerts, 1959); A. Taymans, *L'homme, agent du développement économique* (Louvain, Belgium: Nauwelaerts, 1951); P. de Woot, *La fonction d'entreprise* (Louvain, Belgium: Nauwelaerts, 1962); A. Jacquemin, 'L'entreprise et son pouvoir de marché' (PUF, 1967); P. de Woot and X. Desclée, *Le management stratégique des groupes européens* (Paris: Economica, 1984); J.J. Lambin *Quel avenir pour le capitalisme?* (Dunod, 2011).

4 W.J. Baumol, *The Free Market Innovation Machine* (Princeton University Press, 2002).

Michelin, Renault ... not only evoke the creative individuals who founded them, but companies that have developed the same qualities of vision, of boldness and conviction as their illustrious founders.

Creative ability extends even to larger ensembles. Open or shared innovation strategies make it possible to expand research efforts and accelerate the creation of products, services or processes.

This is particularly true in the areas of information technologies, telecommunications and pharmaceuticals. In the early stages of value creation, cooperation outweighs competition and paves the way for a new culture of collaboration. This enables better control of the increasing complexity of problems and the growing body of knowledge. It undoubtedly lays a more responsible foundation for the development of our creative abilities to meet the challenges of the 21st century.

Driven by competition and technological change, a successful enterprise not only produces and distributes goods and services, it constantly renews them, evolves them, and creates new ones. If one observes performances over a period of five or ten years, there is not one enterprise that has not adapted, transformed and renewed. All have evolved, all have innovated, either in their products or in their markets or processes or their organisation. This reality imbues their work with dynamism and creativity. Indeed, initiative and creativity are central to their actions. As we shall see later, it is they that should articulate the purpose of the business and build its legitimacy.

While being better aware today that the conventional theoretical foundations of our economic model describe only very imperfectly its practical operation,[5] it can be assumed that the entrepreneurial approach of Schumpeter provides a fairly realistic description.

The concepts of *innovation* and *creativity* are essential for our purposes. On their implementation depends the competitiveness of developed countries faced with the dynamism of emerging countries. Over the long term, it is innovation, not just reducing costs and prices that ensures growth and employment. Whether disruptive innovation (new technology, new product . . .) or incremental innovation (increasing quality and developing more high-end products), this is where the comparative advantage of countries with high wages and strong currencies lies. The recent discussion on European competitiveness and the 'fair' value of the euro is an illustration of this. Over the past ten years, each year Germany's trade balance

---

5　See J.P. Hansen, *La vraie nature du marché* (De Boeck, 2012).

had a surplus of over €100 billion (€190 billion in 2012), while that of France was in deficit throughout the period (-€67 billion in 2012).[6] Most economists explain this difference through innovation and high-end quality. For the automobile sector, for example, this was the choice of Germany, while the French positioned themselves in segments which were more sensitive to price factors and currency fluctuations. Respective expenditures on scientific research and technological development reflect and partly explain this difference. This is the kind of reality that must be kept in mind when dealing with the de-industrialisation of Europe and, more generally, the purpose, the *raison d'être* of enterprise.

Although this system has contributed much to the development of the countries that have adopted it, unregulated globalisation is today beginning to show its limitations and dangers.

6 *Sources*: Bloomberg; douanes; COF-REXECODE

1.2 Globalisation and autonomy of economic power

1.2.1 Increasing power of economic players

Companies today are greatly empowered. They control most of the resources of economic creativity: science and technology, finance, organisational, managerial and business skills, networks of relationships, influence, information and communication.

For a growing number of companies, that power is developing on a global scale. The most dynamic stakeholders in globalisation are today's businesses. They were the first to adapt to this evolution and quickly developed effective and efficient international expertise that allows them to systematically exploit these new dimensions. In reality, companies are among the only organisations that have successfully crossed all the major thresholds of globalisation simultaneously—size, time limits, complexity, resources and information. Through their competitive dynamics, companies have adapted more quickly to globalisation that most of our political, social, legal and educative institutions ... This puts them in a strong position to conquer resources, make strategic choices, orientate economic development and control the pace of growth. This gives them real power over the development of countries and regions, and clearly raises the question of their social responsibilities.

A key element of this power is the control of science and technology. Companies have become key players in the orientation of scientific knowledge. It is they who determine its applications. They thus have this famous demiurgic power so much praised and feared by the ancients.

The development and direction of techno-science are often faster than our capacity for institutional or legal change. This runs the risk of making the application of this new knowledge subject to the vagaries of the market rather than directed at certain priority yet unprofitable needs. This can also lead us into situations that have not yet been properly understood by politics or ethics. What must be emphasised at this stage is the danger we face if we are slow to integrate scientific and technical creativity into a more responsible view of our global future, if we abandon techno-sciences to their own dynamics and only competitive logic. Techno-science seized by an incomplete and free economic system, free to impose its choices on us, could lock us into a world where *Brave New World* is just a children's story.[7] This above all involves applications, and we should of course not confuse fundamental research, the free pursuit of truth and its transformation into profits.[8]

The economic stakes of techno-science are enormous: the nano-materials sector, for example, could involve 300,000 to 400,000 direct jobs in Europe, while shale gas is starting to bring about energy independence in the United States, and GMOs (genetically modified organisms) could ensure we can feed a global population approaching 9 billion people . . . But there are also social stakes: the deterioration of the planet threatens hundreds of millions of the poorest people and new technologies could greatly help; some drugs, introduced too quickly, endanger the lives of those who take them, and 'sterile' seeds mean that local farming communities risk losing independence completely; some chemicals and some nanoparticles can affect health, attack bees, destroy biodiversity . . . Political stakes are also important: does the use of military drones by the US administration conform to legal and moral standards in this country? Is the use of cyber counter-espionage to ensure computer secu-

7See on this subject: G. Steiner, *Dans le château de Barbe-Bleue* (Seuil, 1973).
8D. Lambert, *Sciences et théologie* (Lessius, 1999).

rity against hackers sufficiently regulated to prevent espionage by the state?

1.2.2 Power disconnected from politics and ethics

Enterprise being the ultimate agent of economic and technical creativity, it was long believed that its action automatically served the common good through the virtues of the market and its famous 'invisible hand'. Today, this belief is clearly in question. Globalisation, the acceleration of techno-science and the lack of global regulation give the economic system unprecedented autonomy and empowerment. It operates according to its own criteria: profitability, competitiveness, the race to win market share.

At the global level, companies operate in a **political vacuum**. Economic globalisation is advancing much faster than global governance and the necessary regulations. It is beyond the control of the United Nations and gradually imposes its logic on the whole planet. Although economic issues are sometimes over-regulated at the state or European level, they are totally under-regulated globally due to a lack of global governance. This failure by politics to keep up with economics leads to a sort of public powerlessness to drive real development strategies and democratically debate the societal challenges of globalisation. As

Raymond Aron said, nation-states have become too small for the big problems and too big for the small ones. The weakening of states is clearly shown in their failure to address the real challenges of the 21st century, such as climate change, destruction of bio-diversity, rising inequalities . . . It also appears in the increasing difficulty governments face in intervening in the operation of the economy or controlling or tempering its excesses. As discussed below, the weakness of states becomes clear when we look at the desire of industrial or financial lobbies to impose their own standards of conduct or their own scientific expertise in areas such as health and the environment, where risks are difficult to assess. Everything happens as if economic globalisation had been imposed on states, leaving them without even the freedom to choose the type of market economy that suits their country. Thus the Anglo-Saxon model, more financial and less social, tends to gain ground over a more humane model, such as the social market economy, where the Rhineland model is an archetype. The recent closures by multinational companies of some European industrial sites illustrate this failure of states in respect of global strategies that are developed and executed outside of them. Faced with Arcelor Mittal, for example, the French and Belgian governments are almost completely powerless. Although these strategies are often needed for global enterprises, this creates a serious problem because it undermines social cohesion and confidence in their political system. In his last work,[9] Fukuyama reiterates that there is no democracy without the balanced coexistence of a strong state, the rule of law and government accountability. For this author, the decline of civilisations is often explained by the growing strength of interest groups that are beyond political action and can become corrupt. This is what happens when institutions are no longer adapted to reality.

Economic action also takes place in an **ethical vacuum**. Our model operates according to a logic of means and not a logic of ends: it aims to maximise the use of scarce resources and benefits resulting there from. It is based on technical, managerial and financial modernity and not on values. This system is a-moral. In a globalised neoliberal model, 'we can make a lot of money by being irresponsible; incentives for bad behaviour are the strongest'.[10]

An exaggerated example of **instrumental logic** is the answer attributed to the designer Karl Lagerfeld,

9 F. Fukuyama, *Le début de l'histoire. Des origines de la politique à nos jours* (Saint Simon, 2012).
10 H. Mintzberg, 'Rebuilding Companies as Communities', *Harvard Enterprise Review*, 2009.

who was accused of using anorexic women as models, who thus became role models for other young women, that 'the female body needs to adapt to my dresses'.

A more serious example is the dialogue between the boss of Goldman Sachs and the Chairman of the US Senate Committee:

> Your own staff said that this product is 'crap'. You sell it to your customers without informing them, and then you bet against this product. Was there not a conflict of interest?

> In the context of the market, there is no conflict. Everyone chooses the risk he takes.

Another example is the head of TF1 who tells us that the economic base of his job is to create brains available to help Coca-Cola, for example, to sell its product . . . Or the head of an American press group who argues that the difference between a good and a bad newspaper is the difference between yields of 15% and 5%.

While many leaders on a personal level adopt ethical behaviour, the system *in itself* gives no indications other than the markets: effective demand and the requirement of profitability. In an increasing number of cases today, the pressures of the system are stronger than the convictions of those who run it.

Some of them even claim that social responsibilities (CSR) will influence decisions or behaviour only to the extent that the company can find a benefit or legal constraint therein. We are far from ethics. Without ethics and political leadership at a global level, the system tends to be guided only by its instrumental logic.

A Nobel prizewinner in economics, Milton Friedman clearly expresses this idea when he claims that the only social responsibility of business is the enrichment of the shareholder. This primacy of the shareholder reduces the company to its sole financial dimension. It reduces its ethical and political dimensions and leads to it being driven by a tyrannical desire for profit. This primacy of the shareholder is now challenged by a growing number of economists and lawyers. 'What is presented as a model is rather the expression of a value judgment. Its presentation as a principle is a myth'.[11] We should note that most schools of management still teach the same truncated understanding of the role of enterprise.

Beneath the respectable clothing of dynamism and efficiency of open world trade, neoliberal globalisation

11 X. Dieux, 'Droits, pouvoirs et responsabilités des actionnaires et des autres parties prenantes', in X. Dieux and D. Willermain (eds.), *Droit des sociétés?* (ULB, Bruylant, 2012): 7-47.

hides a radical ideology, a single thought. It is, put simply, too absolute a belief in market efficiency as well as an almost visceral distrust of government intervention and regulation of international economic issues. It thus tends to elevate the freedom of the market to apply to means rather than ends. 'Free trade has become a sacrosanct principle of modern economic theory, a universal dogma, a religion whose premise it is forbidden to question'.[12] But it is so reassuring to think that the market economy is a self-regulating process that *automatically* contributes to the common good!

This dominant thinking is not only simplistic and overly optimistic, it is intolerant and arrogant. It is resistant to being challenged and questioned. Those who criticise it are systematically reduced to the rank of utopians, dreamers or pure theorists. Single ways of thinking and power are often linked, then creating the 'arrogance or hypocrisy of social domination and the omnipotence of their implacable determinism' (Bourdieu).

12 M. Allais, Nobel prizewinner, 'La crise intellectuelle du monde occidental. Désagrégation morale', *Le Figaro*, 19 October 2002.

When leaders are locked into a single way of think-ing, they resemble those of the old regime described by Mirabeau: 'Often in error, never in doubt'. Everyone knows that the market economy was a model of efficient growth but, pushed to its limits, this model is becoming a simplistic ideology. The obsessive pursuit of purely technical or financial per-formance in a vacuum removes the ethical and politi-cal dimension from economics. It pushes to the limits the prophetic observation of Montesquieu:

> Among the Greeks and Romans, admiration for political and moral knowledge was elevated to a kind of worship. Today, we have esteem only for the physical sciences . . . and what is good and bad in politics is, among us, a feeling rather than an object of knowledge.

1.3 Unwanted systemic effects, drifts and deviations

Such a situation produces unwanted systemic effects. As Paul Valéry said, 'man often knows what he does, but never knows what does what he does'. Systemic effects not intended by actors are what economists call **externalities**, because they are not required to deal with them. By nature, the instrumental logic of companies also fails to take this into account. When the system is powerful and poorly regulated at a global scale, this attitude can be dangerous. We often assume that our technical, economic and financial systems are fully controllable and that their operators are always rational, prudent and vigilant. The crises we are currently experiencing mean we must be aware that these systems, despite their brilliant achievements, experience drift that amplify collective risks and can lead us into irreversible situations.

The dangers that threaten us are constantly growing. The future of the planet and the survival of the biosphere are in question. The pace of change accelerates and increases the risk of inadequacy, inequality, exclusion, unemployment and social breakdown . . . We have entered into a race where speed is dictated by the dynamics of a global economic system. Change is faster than the adaptation ability of our political, civil, social and educational institutions.

1.3.1 Damage to the planet

Global warming, the depletion of resources and the destruction of biodiversity are obviously not due solely to enterprise. But the economic model that creates exciting lifestyles, travel, new modes of production and distribution, contribute strongly to them. Researchers tell us that we have entered a new geological era, the 'Anthropocene', characterised by the fact that human activity has become capable of influencing geography and climate. Since the industrial revolution, it has even become the main driver of environmental change. The great dispute about the influence of human activity on global warming is being won by those who support the truth of it.

Accelerating its course, our development model is beginning to destroy the planet by depleting its resources, polluting the water and soil and destroying biodiversity. The consequences of climate change will be dramatic—cyclones, tornadoes, tsunamis, desertification, destruction of food resources, famine, displacement . . . And it is the poorest ones who pay the price! Bangladesh could lose 40% of its farmland by 2050. The Intergovernmental Panel on Climate Change (IPCC) says that, by 2050, displacement of 150 million people is likely.[13] The IPCC also tells us that a change in global average temperature of over 4°C above 1990–2000 levels would exceed the adaptive capacity of many ecological processes. At this

13 IPCC, 'Assessing Key Vulnerabilities and the Risk from Climate Change', in *IPCC Fourth Assessment Report: Climate Change* 2007.

point nothing could be done to prevent the loss of some ecosystems, melting glaciers or the disintegration of major ice caps . . .

If we consider the destruction of the seas, the chapter headings alone are enough to make one shudder: pollution and acidification, overfishing and rapid disappearance of fish stocks, changes in wind patterns and ocean currents, destruction of coral reefs and mass extinction of the species that live there . . . Deforestation, acid rain, photochemical smog, species extinction, depletion of groundwater . . . where are we headed?

All these assessments[14] give the same warning: we are endangering our environment and depleting the planet's resources. In 2011, to meet global demand, we consumed 135% of the resources we were entitled to. In other words, we are using our 'natural' capital faster than we can replace it. Ecologically, we are living beyond our means. What will happen when the world population reaches 9 billion people?

1.3.2 Poverty, inequality, precariousness

We all know that the market economy has lifted hundreds of millions of people out of poverty. It has

---

14 EFP (Ecologic Footprint), MEA (Millennium Ecosystem Assessment), PBA (Planetary Boundaries Approach)

managed to create a 'global middle class' and it continues to grow. But there is still a huge global poverty problem. Suffering, and the threats it brings about, are obviously not taken into account by the market, and our creative abilities are insufficiently focused on this global challenge. We need merely to read the list of Millennium Development Goals to remind ourselves: extreme poverty and hunger, child mortality, education, the status of women and maternal health, malaria and AIDS, the environment.

Today, 1.2 billion people struggle to survive on $1.25 a day, and 2.5 billion people on $2. According to the FAO, more than 900 million people suffer from hunger. More than 800 million people have no source of drinking water. According to UNESCO, 2.6 billion people lack access to improved sanitation or available water. Over a billion people in the South are affected by 'orphan' tropical diseases. Between 1975 and 2004, according to a report by *Médecins sans frontières*, of 1,556 drugs developed worldwide, only 18 were intended to treat diseases in poor countries.

On aggregate, inequality is beginning to decrease. But a closer analysis reveals that differences are continuing to widen between the richest and the poorest. Basically, the richest 20% of the world's population has 80% of total revenue, and inequality between these two groups is still widening. While increasing wealth, the market and the invisible hand are unable to ensure equitable distribution. Is there a link between globalisation and rising inequality? The most recent aggregate measures show that the gap between rich and poor countries is beginning to fall, but for the people of these countries, inequalities continue to worsen.[15] In rich countries, inequalities are increasing. These relate not only to income but to all the knowledge and expertise of economic and technical modernity. The division between those who have skills and tools and those who do not extends to almost all areas of life and work: education, adaptability, health, access to networks, jobs . . . One of the major challenges we face is that of reconciling the dynamism of the market economy and social justice.

Many forms of discrimination still exist in business, mainly affecting immigrants and women. The former are especially penalised in terms of hiring and precariousness, the latter in terms of income and also due to their position as mothers. A recent survey showed the reluctance of companies to create more flexible working hours depending on the age of the

15 M. Lundberg and L. Squire, a Report to the World Bank, 1999. See also M. Lundberg and N. Milanovic, 'The Truth about Global Inequality', *Financial Times*, 25 February 2000.

children of working mothers, and to avoid penalising others returning after parental leave.[16]

However, social indicators (health, education, infant mortality . . .) seem to show slow but real change. This suggests that progress is possible when the international political will is able to express itself better and redirect resources in this direction. The major challenge of a globalising society is to implement, at the global level, policies and real means of human development. For the first time in human history, technical, organisational and financial capacity has been sufficiently mastered, accumulated and developed in order to help raise all people out of the simple state of subsistence. The market economy and business managers can therefore contribute but, alone, they will not succeed. Political will is needed: that of transforming our model to ensure a more sustainable and just development.

To this must be added the crisis of **long-term unemployment, insecurity and exclusion**. In industrialised countries, almost a third of the workforce is in a precarious situation. Adjustments to economic cycles weigh very heavily on employees and wage earners:

16 Mouvement Mondial des Mères-Europe, *Ce que les mères veulent,* 2011 Report to the European Parliament.

redundancies, youth unemployment, part-time work, fixed-term contracts . . .

> In contemporary conditions of forced migration and neoliberalism, many people now live without any sense of a secure future, without any sense of political affiliation in the long term, and feeling they are living a kind of half-life, itself an integral part of the daily experience of neoliberalism[17]

Our economic system is not only creative, a driver of dynamic growth and progress, it is also marked by instability, crises and social suffering. More profoundly, an existential approach[18] to this system shows that our development model can also be a force for alienation, an absurd dynamic which has lost the true meaning of existence. The obsession with productivity, headlong competition, loss of autonomy, loss of collective values, has 'led us to believe with Rimbaud that real life is elsewhere'. 'Why should our businesses, which need justify nothing more than creation, so often be destructive to humanity?'[19]

---

17 J. Butler, *Une morale pour temps précaires,* Adorno Prize Acceptance Speech, 11 September 2012.
18 C. Arnsperger, *Critique de l'existence capitaliste* (Paris: Cerf, 2005).
19 X. Grenet, *Cahiers d'un DRH* (Paris: Cerf, 2008).

Precariousness may be such that life becomes unbearable. Can we live life at its best when we are incapable of controlling it?

The recent crisis has led to a resurgence of this precariousness in most European countries, without the indebted public authorities, under the supervision of financial markets and under the constraint of 'competitiveness', seeming to be able to actually help. This increases social divisions and loss of trust in the existing model. It also increases distress and suffering, as is indicated by the growing number of suicides at work.

1.3.3 Weakening of social ties

This is primarily due to the deterioration of relations between capital and labour. Facing closures of plants belonging to multinational corporations, unions are as powerless as the state. Decisions are made 'elsewhere', and dialogue with local managers is devoid of any strategic significance. They can then merely fight rearguard actions. Although in a global sense these decisions are necessary, workers feel like pawns run by robots. Any notion of solidarity disappears between employers and employees in these distant and anonymous games. Trust is broken. When unions, workers and politicians call bosses of multinationals all the names under the sun,[20] leadership, motivation, development and empowerment of staff become hollow concepts. These bosses are seen as 'bastards', 'profiteers' and 'cold monsters'. Indifference and sometimes their statements confirm this picture. Thus, Jack Welch, the former high-performing director of General Electric, said of himself: I am fearless, ruthless and heartless! This confirms the cynicism of Chamfort: 'We govern men with the head; we do not play chess with a good heart'. From this perspective, men are nothing more than pawns in a huge game played outside their control. Such bosses seem indifferent to the suffering of their workers and concerned only with increasing their fortune, which is sometimes spread extravagantly, without restraint. Is it any wonder, then, that there has been an increase in the sense of injustice, and that the social fabric is being torn?

We must add to that the imbalance between the growth of labour income and capital income. In the 30 years that followed the war, an equitable sharing of the fruits of productivity between shareholders

20 In Europe, factory closures by Arcelor Mittal, Peugeot, Ford and Goodyear resulted in an exchange of insults and excess of language: *industrial terrorist, meat slicer, 'crapule', fraud, parasite, pseudo-worker* . . . the same scenario was repeated again and again.

and workers contributed significantly to continued strong growth. There was a kind of social contract. Neoliberal policies have destroyed this balance and, in OECD countries, the share of wages has fallen, in the last 30 years, from 67% to 57% of GDP. As for employment, it is becoming increasingly dependent on global strategies of major private firms and increasingly vulnerable to fluctuations in the global economy. Labour has become the adjustment variable of the profitability of businesses.

The scale and pace of austerity policies imposed at a time of full economic decline, and in a more technocratic than political manner, do not help improve this situation.

This develops **mistrust and the political disengagement of citizens**. The feeling of being subjected to forces they cannot control, forces beyond the power of governments and elected representatives, can only diminish citizens' trust in their institutions and their leaders. They begin to lose their political bearings. They feel threatened in their jobs, their livelihoods, their social protection system, their cultural identity. This creates political disengagement, withdrawal and a widespread individualism. The effects on democracy are deleterious[21] and the 'social contract'

21P. Rosanvallon, *La société des égaux* (Seuil, 2011).

begins to crack. Is it any wonder, then, that we see the rise of populist parties and separatists who refuse European integration?

Some currents go against this trend. These are NGOs and social networks, from which a new political militancy has begun to emerge. But even if they have influence, they lack the effectiveness of the holders of institutional power.

1.3.4 Financial domination

Global finance today comprises a set of markets operating continuously at a global level. Their rules of balance and profitability are imposed on all economic activity. These are markets that constantly evaluate the global economy. It is they that judge the value of major projects. It is they who establish the share price of an enterprise. They also judge the financial stability of governments and the interest rate differential to be paid to compensate for any lack of strength. The financial markets assess international receivables and also set the rate to be used by stakeholders in the system. Finance therefore oversees all economic activity. Today it is in a dominant position for the assessment and guidance of our growth and development strategies, with control of the economic system gradually transferring from entrepreneurs to financiers. This financial domination can contribute to making entrepreneurship subordinate to the hazards of speculation. Speculative bubbles and the current crisis are recent examples.

> We talk about financial markets as if they were rational and stable. If they were able to produce accurate estimates of values and prices, their role would be useful. The problem is that this is not the case. They are, from this viewpoint, very different from goods markets. These deal with actual goods, having a value that consumers can judge, while financial markets are based on subjective wagers, speculation. These are markets of promises. They buy and sell expectations. Their logic is mimetic in nature—each investor takes a position based on what others will do ... The financial market is a deeply erratic and inconsistent sovereign.[22]

Insofar as the financial markets are inefficient and operate on the basis of an ideology unsuited to sustainable development, their domination is a real political problem. If we add to this the invention of more complex and less readable financial instruments, the risk of drift increases.

22 A. Orléan, *Le marché domine*, interview in *Le Monde*, 21 January 2012. See also: *Manifeste des économistes atterrés* (Editions Les Liens qui libèrent, 2010).

To grow their business and spread their risks, banks have continued to create new financial instruments, including derivatives, securities whose price evolves according to the price of another asset (oil, interest rates, shares . . .). Some are fixed (forwards, futures, swaps), others optional (options and warrants). These products are not all very readable and often involve increasingly risky gambles. As discussed below, some banks have used them to the detriment of their customers. Some financial products are so complex that they can create widespread uncertainty, mainly because nobody knows exactly where they are. The widespread diffusion of CDS (credit default swaps), for example, is driving states to ruin to save banks with systemic risks that have become too important. Other products can be toxic, that is to say nobody wants to buy them anymore, which was the case for US subprime mortgages. Widely disseminated by the financial markets, they escaped out of control and were the cause of the 2008 crisis.

As one former banker said, the combination of greed and intelligence is a source of some current banking excesses. These led the economy into a speculative race where money was used to create more money without investing in the production of goods or services useful to people.

Should we evoke the world of hedge funds and 'alternative management', which seek gains disconnected from the overall evolution of markets: short selling of shares and currency exchange, investment leveraged through hedge funds?

If we add the 'mad' traders that plagued several major banks, causing them to lose considerable sums, we can only worry about the culture that dominates financial institutions. A recent study by the University of St Gallen[23] compared the behaviour of 28 professional traders with those of a sample of psychopaths in a mental hospital. The tests focused on the ability to cooperate and egotism. The results exceeded initial assumptions: traders were more aggressive, determined to destroy the enemy, more manipulative and less scrupulous than psychopaths. Is it any wonder then that these traders have abused the system by speculating and manipulating the markets in the hope of generating greater short-term profits?

More generally, we should be aware of the danger represented today by the inconsiderate requirement of maximum profit for shareholders imposed by the dominant financiers. We risk seeing the spirit of speculation outweighing the spirit of enterprise and diverting it from its true function: real economic

23 P. Sherrer and T. Noll, Université de Saint Gallen, 2012.

progress. The danger grows of seeing entrepreneurs inhibited or 'doped' in their plans by external analysis underestimating or overestimating the shares of their business.

1.3.5 Behavioural drift

When speculation outweighs entrepreneurship, we risk slipping into a casino economy where behaviour is all too often that of greed and excess: delusional requirements of profitability and growth, misleading figures, falsehoods when selling financial products, lies about tobacco, asbestos, fertilisers, seed, food, drugs . . . , illegal deforestation, illegal overfishing . . . excess in external growth strategies, excesses in executive pay . . .

Drift increases: manipulation of accounts, concealment of debts, tax engineering, insider trading, toxic products, corruption, breach of trust . . . Hubris, harassment, spying, discrimination . . . Abuse of power, cartels, unlawful agreements and other conspiracies . . .

The indifference of the financial community to their own excesses is worrying. Resistance and lobbying to prevent any significant reform is one sign of this. Good conscience prevails: 'I am only a banker doing God's job . . .'[24] while some financiers do not hesitate to cheat, lie, manipulate Libor and Euribor interbank rates . . . black money, hiding the extent of the Greek debt, incitement to purchase rotten shares, undervaluation of risky positions, irresponsible lending . . . to the point of being called 'banksters' and 'sewer banks'. According to the SEC (Securities and Exchange Commission), Goldman Sachs got rid of its subprime mortgages by selling them to its customers. Barclays deceived the whole financial community by cheating on Libor, and a dozen other major banks, such as Société Générale and Crédit Agricole were involved in it. Deutsche Bank is accused by the Frankfurt public prosecutor of aiding tax evasion, and Standard Chartered accused of fraudulent transactions with Iran. HSBC, in 2012, set aside €1.6 billion to cope with future fines . . . We should recall the guilty tolerance, if not encouragement, of several banks concerning 'mad' speculators. Each day the press announces a new financial or banking scandal. The worldwide tax avoidance scheme that has just been revealed by Offshore Leaks should make us cautious, if not sceptical, of the ethical claims of the business world.

24 Lloyd Blankfein, head of Goldman Sachs

Should we also mention the dishonest lobbying, strategies aimed at casting doubt on the dangers that threaten us, resistance to any regulation, the organised 'sale' of climate, food and health scepticism, and the refusal of a reasonable use of the precautionary principle?

Should we add corruption, espionage, incestuous collusion with the public authorities? After the *News of the World* affair, a member of the British parliamentary committee said that James Murdoch 'was the first mafia head to not know he ran a criminal enterprise'.

Such deviations belong to the realm of excess, lies and cheating. They typically involve human weakness. For the sake of reality we should remember that they are not new and we do not live in a perfect world. Aristophanes, suffering from the corruption and decay that prevailed in Athens, asked even then if anyone knew where he could buy a nose without holes. However, given the proliferation of scandals, one may wonder if it is just a moral failure of a few leaders and financiers or, more profoundly, a real flaw in the capitalist system. Such slippage is often induced by the systemic aberrations described above. It may suggest that, insofar as the systems are lightly regulated, the risk increases of seeing flaws expand and more of this kind of drift. Is it utopian to want to improve an economic system some of whose key players are charged with conspiracy, aggravated fraud, embezzlement, misuse of company property, conspiracy, fraud, etc.?

Faster change, a purely market-driven approach to business, financial domination, despite some behavioural drift, have created a society richer than before, there is no doubt, but also a political inability to solve problems in the long-term, cultural insecurity, collective irresponsibility concerning undesirable consequences and a development model lacking any ethical or political dimensions.

The globalisation of our business model and the acceleration of techno-sciences bring us both many opportunities and many threats.[25] But in the absence of an adequate governance system, malfunctions will become more frequent, deeper and more visible. A sort of anxiety starts to set in, and the legitimacy of economic power is questioned. The most serious danger is the increasing decoupling of economics, politics and ethics.

25 See, particularly, the balanced analysis of the future of capitalism by J.J. Lambin, 2011, op. cit.
      See also B. Collomb and M. Drancourt, *Plaidoyer pour l'entreprise* (François Bourdin Editeur, 2010).

The challenges we face are growing. The future of the planet and the survival of humanity are in question while many of us continue to trust in the economic system, seemingly unaware that radical change is necessary and urgent. Do we not resemble 'the man who refused to believe they had set fire to his house because he had the key in his pocket' (Tocqueville)?

Let us not delude ourselves. We are on the brink of abyss. We are moving towards ever more severe crises, the consequences of which will be disastrous. Let us stop following the herd and bleating in unison about the merits of an unbridled market economy and, especially, participating without trying to fundamentally transform.

But the complexity and uncertainty that are the hallmarks of the evolution of a globalised system mean that we need to take a modest approach to change. The key is to start it, and involve the largest number of political, economic and social stakeholders . . . International regulation is necessary, but without global governance it will emerge neither easily nor quickly. The shift towards a model of more sustainable and fair development can only be achieved through a tentative and multifaceted approach. The purpose of this essay is to suggest that companies can play an important role if they adopt a more responsible culture. But alone, they will not succeed, and neither is this desirable.

To achieve this, we can draw on the concept of metamorphosis used by Edgar Morin, by reference to the transformation of the caterpillar into a butterfly. The metamorphosis is as radical as revolution (becoming a butterfly is not a trivial transformation or mere good practice), but unlike the revolution, it keeps what was good in the old system (life, vitality and its potential). In the case of the caterpillar, it is interesting to note that, without metamorphosis, it would be incapable of reproduction, and therefore lasting.

2

Rethinking the purpose of business

If we want to avoid the current drifts becoming global disasters, it is imperative to restore the ethical and political dimension to economics.

In a world where so many organisations and so many people no longer have a clear direction, should we not rethink the purpose of enterprise and, above and beyond mere means, return to aims. We are here in the field of meaning.

Defining the purpose, the *raison d'être*, of enterprise, means agreeing to place its operation in the broader context of ethics and the common good, without which it has no political or moral legitimacy.

This is ultimately to recognise that enterprise is not an end in itself, and serves a public interest that goes beyond it alone. Let's attempt it by focusing on what is specific about enterprise.

2.1 Economic creativity: specific function of business enterprise

The *raison d'être* of the business firm should be anchored in its specific function. This specificity, we have seen, is defined in terms of initiative, creativity and innovation in economic, technical and organisational fields.[26] In these areas, its action is fundamentally entrepreneurial.

As mentioned before, if high-performing enterprises are observed over a period of five or ten years, there is not one that has not adapted, transformed and renewed. All have evolved, innovated in all their products, their markets, their processes or in their organisation. This reality imbues their work with dynamism and creativity.

---

26 P. de Woot, *Should Prometheus Be Bound? Corporate Global Responsibility* (Palgrave-Macmillan, 2005, 2009); see also: *Spirituality and Business. A Christian Viewpoint* (GSE Research Ltd, 2013).

In a market system economy, an enterprise is the very agent of economic and technical creativity. It is enterprise that implements it and gives it concrete form. It does not restrict itself to describing, it enacts it and implements it.[27] To do this, the successful company has entrepreneurial and innovative qualities that are often deployed on a global scale. It knows that its success and survival depend on these qualities. It supports the basic intuition of Schumpeter that *being an entrepreneur means changing an existing order.* Initiative and creativity are central to entrepreneurship. This is what justifies its freedom and gives its actions their historical dimension.

A good eulogy of this creativity can be found in the Greek myths. The creators of material progress are given a key role. They are gods, titans and heroes.

Let us pause for a moment on that extraordinary meditation on the grandeur of the entrepreneur and the meaning of his actions. Prometheus is one of the great myths. This Titan has all the characteristics of the entrepreneur: he *sees* the progress that mortals could achieve with fire, he took the *risk* of stealing it from the gods, he has the energy to do so and to *convince*

27 It is significant that the Littré defines enterprise as *the implementation of a project.* 'What we imagine, we can make happen' proclaims General Electric, the American giant.

men to use it.[28] It is the same for Hephaestus (Vulcan), the father of the arts of the fire. He manufactures tools, weapons and jewellery. He is a god. Ulysses is a hero, whose Odyssey describes the commercial success of the Greeks in the Mediterranean. He is the marketing man of antiquity—clever, bold, enterprising . . . Ulysses of the 'thousand tricks'. Jason pursues wealth, the golden fleece. The myth is clear—with his Argonauts, he began to explore the Black Sea and the sources of this precious metal. Hercules is the myth of development. He shines less brightly than Prometheus but will become a god. Finally, Icarus brings us back to full technical progress, accomplishing the age-old human dream of flying like a bird.

Chained to his rock, Prometheus talks about his works and, for the first time in a beautiful paean, he sings of entrepreneurship and innovation:

> Still, listen to the miseries that beset mankind—
> how they were witless before and I made them
> have sense and endowed them with reason . . .
>
> One day in the sacred fennel stalk,
>
> I stored the spark . . .
>
> I bestowed upon them liberating fire,
>
> O creative source

28 As we have seen, these are the rare qualities that Schumpeter attributes to modern entrepreneurs.

Teacher to mortals,

A means to mighty end . . .

First of all, though they had eyes to see, they saw to no avail; they had ears, but they did not understand; but, just as shapes in dreams, throughout their length of days, without purpose they wrought all things in confusion. They had neither knowledge of houses built of bricks and turned to face the sun nor yet of work in wood; but dwelt beneath the ground like swarming ants, in sunless caves. They had no sign either of winter or of flowery spring or of fruitful summer, on which they could depend but managed everything without judgment, until I taught them to discern the risings of the stars and their settings, which are difficult to distinguish. Yes, and numbers, too, chiefest of sciences, I invented for them, and the combining of letters, creative mother of the Muses' arts, with which to hold all things in memory.

I, too, first brought brute beasts beneath the yoke to be subject to the collar and the pack-saddle, so that they might bear in men's stead their heaviest burdens; and to the chariot I harnessed horses and made them obedient to the rein, to be an image of wealth and luxury. It was I and no one else who invented the mariner's flaxen-winged car that roams the sea . . .

> Hear the rest and you shall wonder the more at the arts and resources I devised. This first and foremost: if ever man fell ill, there was no defence—no healing food, no ointment, nor any drink—but for lack of medicine they wasted away, until I showed them how to mix soothing remedies with which they now ward off all their disorders . . . Now as to the benefits to men that lay concealed beneath the earth—bronze, iron, silver, and gold—who would claim to have discovered them before me? No one, I know full well, unless he likes to babble idly. Hear the sum of the whole matter in the compass of one brief word—every art possessed by man comes from Prometheus. He who rescued the men did not find the path to salvation.[29]

What greater epic than that of economic and technical progress?

And what pride its actors must feel!

Marx himself was amazed at this capacity 'in the course of barely secular class domination, the capitalist bourgeoisie has accomplished wonders far surpassing Egyptian pyramids, Roman aqueducts, and Gothic cathedrals . . .'[30] He added: 'it has conducted

---

29 Aeschylus, *Prometheus Bound*, trans. A. Bonnard (Lausanne: Mermod, 1946).

30 K. Marx, *The Communist Party Manifesto* (Brussels, 1848).

expeditions that put in the shade all former: exoduses of nations and crusades'.

Entrusted with this creative work, how have business leaders let finance reduce their purpose to solely creating profit for shareholders? How did they let it dominate the 'real' economy, which is the true place of creation of material progress and the source of their social legitimacy? How have they thought so little about the purpose of their action? How have they failed to give their business a more dynamic and exciting vision based on their creativity and contribution to economic progress?

2.2 Ambiguity of economic and technical creativity

In Greek myths, the creators of material progress are heroes, titans and gods, but they are also cursed: Odysseus cannot return home, Jason loses his children, killed by Medea, Hercules is burned in the tunic of Nessus, Icarus crashed and Vulcan is lamed and deceived. Why are they cursed? Echoing through the centuries, this question is as relevant today.

From the outset, the incredible series of innovations from the Neolithic period onwards is presented in terms of human progress. But the other side of technical creation is fear: fear of consequences and questions about the meaning, limits and dangers of the unbridled use of these new tools.

A Chinese myth is clear on this point. In ancient times, blacksmiths became kings when they made the greatest and most beautiful bronze vase. After ten years, they had to produce another which surpassed it in beauty. For the vase to be perfect, they had to throw themselves into the furnace with their wife. The Chinese thus limited the power of the demiurges they considered dangerous. They had admiration for these masters of the art, but also fear of their power! The myth says that the kings soon realised that the wife alone would suffice to make the perfect vase, and so they kept their life and power.[31]

In *Prometheus Bound*, Aeschylus also challenges us with the ambiguity of purposeless creativity and unlimited entrepreneurial power. For masters of technical creation, the temptation of excess, hubris, is constantly present. Prometheus is seized with it. The gods thus chained him to a rock where, every morning, an eagle fed on his liver.

31 M. Granet, *La civilisation chinoise*, Bibliothèque de l'Évolution de l'Humanité (Albin Michel, 1968).

> My name is clairvoyant, he who knows, Pro-
> metheus the subtle . . . deliverer of men . . . I
> freed man from the pangs of death

And when the chorus of the Oceanides, surprised by this extraordinary statement, asked him: 'what remedy found'st thou for this malady?' He answers, 'I planted blind hope in the heart of him'.
Blindness!
Confronted by the acceleration of sciences and technologies, George Steiner asks the same question.[32] Unlike art, he says, science works by accumulation, and development becomes exponential. It gradually goes beyond the realm of democratic debate. By their magnitude and speed, science and technology have gained their own dynamics and an independence that could lead them on a dangerous path.

> Any definition of a post-classical civilization
> must learn to count on scientific knowledge
> and the world of mathematic and symbolic
> languages. Because they alone are omnipotent:
> in fact as well as in the fever of progress that
> defines us . . .

32 G. Steiner, *Dans le château de Barbe-Bleue. Note pour une
   redéfinition de la culture* (Gallimard, 1986).

Isabelle Stengers takes up this theme and suggests that science should agree to question its purpose and its role in society.[33]

The application of science and the focus of techniques are evidently not neutral. 'With his ingenious knowhow, exceeding all expectation, his robust power to create sometimes brings evil, at other times, excellence' (Sophocles).

A few examples will suffice to illustrate this point.

Biogenetics promise abundant harvests, solutions to incurable diseases, longer lives and less decay . . . But they also raise the spectre of genetic manipulations with unpredictable consequences, affecting the very nature of humans and all living species.

Nuclear technology can better diagnose diseases, cure some cancers and preserve food, medical instruments . . . It provides cheap energy and does not pollute the atmosphere, but its waste is a long-term threat that we still don't know how to dispose of. It can become a formidable deterrent in the hands of governments and the military, but also a tool of blackmail and terror in the hands of extremists or 'rogue

33 I. Stengers, *Une autre science est possible, manifeste pour un ralentissement des sciences* (La Découverte, 2012).

states'. Man now faces the possibility of destroying his own kind.

The Internet and media open new vistas of information, interactive communication, exchange, debate and education. They could create the 'noosphere' so dear to Teilhard de Chardin and help the advent of a world united in diversity. But they also bring with them the possibility of a world subject to information overload, simplifications, ratings figures, confinement into narrow specialisations or avatars. They can also globalise threats to security, criminal networks and the ad nauseam broadcasting of violent images. They also force us to rethink some basic concepts such as the protection of privacy, which the sale of personal data for marketing purposes already fails to respect. As we know now, *big data* is not far from *big brother.*

The ambiguity of technological innovations has created, in the public mind, widespread fear and often excessive mistrust of possible 'progress'. Everything related to food, health, the environment or security is marked by anxiety and a lack of objective information. We will see later that the lack of public expertise, and doubt and misinformation strategies conducted by some companies make it difficult to hold any serious debate on a reasonable application of the famous precautionary principle.

We should be aware of the dangers of an unbridled Promethean system finding its legitimacy solely in its technical superiority, which would be tempted by the 'unlimited', and whose delusional optimism could make us believe that it alone can solve all our problems. We must remember that although the world received the material progress from Prometheus, it was given neither justice nor wisdom, which are gifts of Zeus himself.[34]

This is where corporate responsibility comes in. In fact, the power of corporations, especially over science and technology, is huge. Cut off from any ethical and political dimension, it can become threatening.[35] They are therefore responsible for giving a meaning to their creativity and putting it into the service of the common good and the development of human dignity.

34 F. Flahault, *Le crépuscule de Prométhée, Contribution à une histoire de la démesure humaine* (Mille et une nuits, 2008).

35 J. van Rijckevorsel, *L'entreprise, un moteur de progrès?* (Thélès, 2012).

2.3 Transforming creativity into progress

Questioning the purpose of enterprise and the development model it follows is to question material progress, its focus and its ambiguities. If leaders want the extraordinary *creativity* of enterprise to translate into *progress* for humanity, they have a duty to orientate it, to give it meaning by restoring its ethical and political dimensions. Is not economic progress a more serious foundation than mere profit for rethinking enterprise and giving meaning to its actions? Is it not a more serious foundation than merely quantitative growth? A growing number of economists[36] are calling into question growth and its measurement, GDP. They put forward more refined economic goals, such as sustainable development, different growth, prosperity without growth, green and social economics, solidarity . . . They also propose using other criteria

36 See I. Cassiers *et al.*, *Redéfinir la prospérité. Jalons pour un débat public* (L'Aube, 2011); T. Jackson, *Prospérité sans croissance* (De Boeck/Etopia, 2010). See also works on growth and 'happiness', particularly B. Frey and A. Stutzer, *Happiness and Economics* (Princeton University Press, 2002). See also R. Gaucher, Bonheur et économie (L'Harmattan, 2009); R. Layard, G. Mayraz and S.J. Nickell, *The Marginal Utility of Income* (CEPDP, 784; Centre for Economic Performance, London School of Economics and Political Science, 2007).

and other performance measures such as, for example, the Human Development Index added to many other indicators: ecological footprint, the 'better life', 'real progress', etc.

Questioning the purpose of enterprise and the development model it follows to question material progress, its focus and its ambiguities. Giving enterprise a purpose means, particularly, reflecting on and answering the following questions:

Economic and technical creativity:
- Why?
- For whom?
- How?

The answers to these questions can only be ethical and political.

While the economic system is amoral, its stakeholders cannot be, without becoming irresponsible. Defining the *raison d'être* of the enterprise therefore means including its specific kind of creativity within the broader context of human activities.

We must stop pretending that there is a quasi-automatic convergence between current economic creativity and the overall development of humanity. We must stop claiming that only self-interest should guide economic behaviour and that, to respond to global challenges, we should just trust the technical ingenuity of people and market indicators. Business will only be responsible if it places its specific function within the context of the sustainable human development view.

From this viewpoint, we propose defining the purpose of enterprise as follows: *the creation of economic and social progress in a sustainable and globally responsible manner.*[37]

Let us reiterate that economics is merely a subset and cannot dominate society to impose its limited vision of progress. Other forms of progress exist in the cultural, social, political, spiritual and educational realms . . . While economic progress favours some of them, however, we cannot pretend that it covers the entire field of human progress. We have also seen that the excesses of the current system could lead to regression and destructive situations.

If there is no longer automatic convergence between economic growth and the common good, entrepreneurs, individually or collectively, become responsible for the meaning and purpose of their action. This must be tailored to fit the progress of humanity rather than follow a purely financial logic or a growth

37 Global Responsible Leadership Initiative, *A Call to Action* (Bruxelles, 2005).

logic which has no other purpose than its own benefit. From such a perspective, profit appears more as a constraint of shareholder remuneration and long-term survival. It cannot be presented as the purpose of the company. It is an issue of means rather than aims. From the legal point of view, the profit motive is that of any commercial company. This is true for shareholders but as they are not the only stakeholder, the purpose of the company cannot be reduced to this single measure. Value for the shareholder is merely one of many measures of economic performance, and the company cannot be reduced to this single dimension. This approach also calls into question the concept of purely quantitative growth and its measurement merely by gross domestic product (GDP).

3
A responsible entrepreneurial culture

Faced with criticism of our development model and calls for its transformation, many economists agree, ironically, saying all this may be true, but what are you going to substitute for an economic system which is now known to be the most effective wealth creation system? This essay suggests that it is less an issue of changing the mechanisms of the system and risking losing its creativity than encouraging its leaders to look at aims as much as means. It is less an issue of transforming structures than changing the culture, and then the guidelines. Let's reiterate—it's a case of restoring the ethical and political dimensions to economic activity, which is the only way for business leaders to confront the complexity of reality. Let's once and for all leave behind the narrow ideology of Milton Friedman who dared to claim that the only social responsibility of business is to maximise profit for shareholders ... This short-sighted view profoundly influenced neoliberal thinking, and we must reject it.

Culture is the set of symbolic systems used to produce social interactions.[38] It is part of the intrinsic nature of human societies. Situated between psyche and reality, its symbolic nature gives it a different dimension to merely technical approaches alone or simple instrumental rationality.

Culture is an organic process that mobilises the entire organisation. It represents, to some extent, the genes of the company. It contains the values that will guide its decisions, behaviour and climate of the whole organisation. Some companies have made this an explicit part of their approach, and presented it as a way of being: the Danone way, the HP way ... The culture is then their 'soft power'. It is at this level that change is sustainable. It is also at this level that

---

38 T. De Smedt, *Les nouvelles techniques médiatiques imposent-elles une nouvelle culture ?*, Presentation to the Royal Academy of Belgium, 2 February 2013.

resistance to change is strongest. Major scandals such as Enron,[39] the banks,[40] the tobacco industry, etc. can be explained more by corporate culture than merely by the 'criminal' behaviour of one or another of its leaders.

If profit is not the sole criterion of economic decisions, what other criteria should be added to change corporate culture? Going beyond merely criteria, it is a broader dimension, a rediscovered depth, a return to moral and civic responsibility. It may be suggested that the strategic decisions of the company continue to be constrained by profit but address ethical and political issues that transform the creative economy

39 Enron ('the crooked E') is a typical example of this cultural drift. Analyses have shown that the pillaging of resources of this company was organised by a 'clique' of 150 dominating and intimidating managers. Their idea of power was to impose their views unilaterally, to ignore different opinions and impose a financial 'star system'. Recent banking investigations and procedures suggest the same thing. This is also the case with the four Ryanair pilots who called into question the very culture of their company.

40 'Why did nobody, within Goldman Sachs, say: "What we are doing is obscene"?', M. Lewis, *The Big Short: Inside the Doomsday Machine* (Norton, 2010). In recent big scandals, the corporate culture was generally called into question. This was the case with Enron, Société Général (Kerviel) and Goldman Sachs (Greg Smith, denouncing a toxic and destructive working environment).

into progress and give it its social legitimacy. These questions are not meant to destroy the system but restore full responsibility to those who control it. This critical distance, both ethical and political, allows them to take a broader and new approach to the goals and guidelines of the economic game.

3.1 Restoring ethical and civic dimensions to corporations

3.1.1 Back to ethics

If a corporation wants to give its actions meaning, if it wants to transform its economic creativity into progress and place it within the context of other forms of human progress, the ethical dimension is as essential as the political dimension in informing and guiding their choices and behaviour.

The ethics of responsibility require one to commit, to choose a direction, to decide to transform fate into a destiny chosen by us. This is an ongoing critical reassessment[41] to avoid becoming a 'pebble tossed by the waves' or a mere relay of an all-powerful system.

41 G. de Stexhe, *Cours d'éthique 2007* (Bruxelles: Facultés Universitaires saint Louis, 2007).

It is a constant retort to the unacceptable. This 'must be expressed and be consolidated every day. Every time a Creon appears, an Antigone must be reborn'.[42]

Enlightened by values, the ethics of responsibility take into account not only behaviour itself but the consequences of decisions and actions. Intentions are not enough. The consequences of action must be taken into account.

A central ethical issue is that of human suffering. *Ethics begins at the first cry of human suffering.*[43] They prevent us from being indifferent to the suffering of others, especially if it is we who have caused it.

When the jury of the 2012 Nobel Prize for Economics tells us that it decided to return to the foundations of economic thought, namely the theory of the motivating forces of human action, one feels concerned. When one of the winners[44] professes that 'every human act can be analysed as an exchange, based on

---

42 D. Lambert, *Sciences et théologie* (Bruxelles: Lessius, 1999). See also P.F. Smets, *Ethique ou cosmétique? Le retour des valeurs dans un monde paradoxal* (Bruxelles: Bruylant, 2002).

43 See C. Fourez, *La construction des sciences. Introduction à la philosophie et à l'éthique des sciences* (De Boeck, 1988).

44 Alvin Roth

a calculation of maximising interest, whether financial, moral or aimed at seeking fame', one wonders about this conception of morality. What do we mean when we invoke 'moral interest'? Ethics 'by interest' is not ethics. Ethics is essentially disinterested. And then, how restrictive for economic action to be reduced to 'maximising value' measured by profit! Can one really reduce the ability to initiate and innovate to this point? Doesn't this mean cutting it off completely from all ethics? Should the creative act of the entrepreneur really be reduced to his own interest? Many say that money is not their primary reason, but rather the challenge or usefulness of innovation. Is the quality of human relationships within a company limited merely to profit? Anybody who sets out such a simplistic idea can never have studied an organisation. They can never have met real leaders if they reduce them to mechanical agents for maximising profit. Not all bosses are like Jack Welch, CEO of General Electric, nicknamed 'Neutron Jack' because, like the neutron bomb, he sacrificed workers rather than equipment. When companies focus their creativity on the poorest, towards the 'bottom of the pyramid', there is undoubtedly a certain amount of self-interest but also a desire for solidarity that is more than a mere calculation.

We must therefore ask ourselves if we should not reduce the importance of the market and its invisible hand and open an ethical debate on a broader and deeper basis than that of the economy alone. Entrusting this reflection to economists is to risk misunderstanding the true nature of ethics. The pursuit of self-interest alone can only produce calculating robots that are unable to, on their own, give an ethical and political dimension to their work. Added to this is the fact that the concept of interest described as 'a motivating source of human activity' is even more vague and less readable than the concept of utility. It is one of those constructions of the economic theory that are so cut off from reality. People and organisations are more complex than economic models. We must be consistent: we cannot claim to be responsible and be merely robots of instrumental performance.

Fortunately , another Economics Nobel prizewinner, Amartya Sen, a specialist in extreme poverty, rejects any abstract view of the individual, thus reviving more practical ethics,[45] like that of the *shared humanity* of Hannah Arendt, for example or the *realistic utopia of human rights* of Habermas. Let's work

---

45 See the analysis of Martha Nussbaum, *Creating Capabilities. The Human Development Approach* (Harvard University Press, 2011).

towards the existence of *a universal morality based on the ideas of humanity and reason*.[46]

Perhaps one of the first steps in a truly ethical approach would be moving beyond a state of indifference to anything that is not directly efficiently instrumental and listen to the cries of those that our economic system causes to suffer. Indifference makes us deaf and blind. It is a denial of humanity. But 'the market economy will only be sustainable if it is social and redistributive'.[47]

If ethics begin at the first cry of human suffering, should we not listen to the clamour of those that our model of development, our instrumental logic, our one-track way of thinking cause to suffer in one way or another? Listen to them directly when possible, or their advocates, who are more numerous by the day.

We must go further and assume, as far as possible, responsibility for the future we are implementing. According to Bergson, consciousness is a link between what was and what will be; a bridge between the past and the future.[48] This clearly concerns the

---

46 L'instruction morale à l'école, circulaire du Ministère de l'Education nationale, Paris, August 2011.

47 B. Colmant, *Les sentinelles de l'économie* (Anthemis, 2012).

48 H. Bergson, *Les deux sources de la morale et de la religion* (Presses universitaires de France, 1932).

planet. It also concerns the unique and difficult questions raised by the endless discoveries of science.

3.1.2 Back to citizenship and the 'political'

The real political question of our time is that of *the type of world we want to build together with the tremendous resources and immense capabilities we have at our fingertips.* It concerns the common good and not the sole interest of shareholders, a question at a different level from that of growth or profit. It does not mean questioning the dynamism and creativity of our model but rather the use made of it. It means reflecting on the type of development that is desirable, and the direction of our creative capacity. Stuck in linear time, humans are historical beings and their actions build the world. They are responsible for the society they create. This responsibility is all the greater for business leaders that wield such creativity and power.

The United Nations propose the concept of sustainable development. This new model sketches out a real project for the future aimed at returning economic action to the context of the global common good.

Its definition is well-known, that of the Brundtland Report:[49] 'Sustainable development is development that meets the needs of the present without compromising the ability of future generations to meet their own needs'.

This is the outline of a very different concept of development, growth and prosperity.

Companies cannot ignore this debate. They are called upon to take part in dialogue with other stakeholders in society. They cannot ignore the need, indeed urgent, to transform the system they control. Should they not participate in governance processes emerging in this area?

3.2 Areas of progress: entrepreneurship, leadership, statesmanship

Real cultural change drives leaders to rethink three major business functions: creativity and innovation (**entrepreneurship**), organising and leading a community (**leadership**) and serving the common good (**statesmanship**). We are not here to discuss in detail each of these functions, but to outline some practical

49 UN, *Notre avenir à tous* (Les éditions du fleuve, Montréal, 1989).

pathways for change to begin to restore the ethical and political dimensions to economics.

3.2.1 Entrepreneurship: the entrepreneur, creator of progress and not just profit

It's time to get back to basics: enterprising. Enterprises must be an agent of progress before being a dividend machine. It's not finance, it's the capacity for initiative and innovation that is the engine of economic development. In the long term, it is through their creativity that corporations provide material progress, but also employment and the competitiveness of regions, countries and continents. The real winning strategies are those that rely on the ability to enact long-term initiatives based on investments in research and development, technical, managerial and organisational skills, qualified, creative and motivated staff . . . This is where the keys to economic development lie.

If we want corporations to fully assume their societal responsibilities, it is also time to better focus their role as entrepreneurs. It is through this entrepreneurial capacity that they serve the common good. It is therefore important to rethink the direction of their creative force and their ability to correct the excesses of the system they drive. How can a company that wants to become responsible contribute, with others, to solving the global problems of the 21st century? In the most critical areas of our growth model, how can it become part of the solution rather than the problem?

What is new today is the emergence of *new forms of innovation* and new fields of entrepreneurship. Corporations are at the origin of many of these developments, while others come from civil society. All reflect a deep sense of initiative and the specific qualities of the classic entrepreneur: vision, risk-taking and conviction. They offer exciting and dynamic opportunities for the establishment of an alternative development model. These emerging initiatives are neither rivals nor exclusive, but complementary. They indicate new pathways for responsible innovation and cooperation and collective action in the public interest. They also embody a type of leadership that develops the creativity of all members of the organisation. They are the premises of a change in our societies towards greater corporate responsibility. This 'creative bubbling' (Edgar Morin) opens up new areas of responsibility.

3.2.1.1 The corporate social responsibility movement

Many actions have been taken in this direction, many initiatives have already emerged. Business CSR networks have been created to respond specifically to certain system malfunctions, including environmental issues, poverty and inequality. This is particularly true of Corporate Social Responsibility Europe, created by Etienne Davignon, which includes several hundred large corporations. In partnership with the European Commission, the network attempts to define the future of the responsible corporation. This is also true of the World Business Council for Sustainable Development, chaired by Bertrand Collomb, and the United Nations Global Compact launched by Kofi Annan.

When those corporations declare themselves to be responsible, and proclaim it publicly, should we take them seriously? Are we merely dealing with slogans, wishful thinking and public image or are we already seeing an emerging reality and concrete actions?

The first concrete achievements are beginning to be seen, and some of them are convincing. The CSR Europe database presents more than 600 'best practices' of its members.[50] For some of them, we are clearly beyond mere public relations pitches. Three

50 CSR Europe, www.csreurope.org.

main lines of action should be highlighted: the development of products or services that meet the expectations of stakeholders; the establishment of internal processes and new skills to measure and limit the negative effects that their actions can have on the environment or society; and increased participation in improving the quality of life of local communities.[51]

All this is moving in the right direction but we must go further. Many companies still limit their approach to a few, very fragmented actions. If the corporate social responsibility movement is limited to a few 'best practices' without changing culture and attitudes, it does not become a transformative force and will not be taken seriously by other societal stakeholders. If it is merely sticking new labels on old practices, it will be limited to 'cleaning out the Augean stables with a toothpick'.

3.2.1.2 Towards an improved development model

Questioning our growth model has opened up new opportunities for creative entrepreneurs, offering a host of opportunities that can restore the ethical and political dimensions to their actions. While some

---

51   F. Maon, V. Swaen and A. Lindgreen, 'Designing and Implementing Corporate Social Responsibility', *Journal of Business Ethics* 87 Suppl. 1 (April/May 2009).

company managers continue to work within the existing model, some are also starting to go beyond it.

One of the most clearly articulated models in terms of environment and resources is that proposed by Jeremy Rifkin[52] under the name of the **circular economy**. Starting from the assumption that the scarcity of resources is becoming a major global problem, it proposes *a culture of productivity of natural resources.* This would play an equally strategic role as labour productivity and thereby direct the creativity of corporations towards meeting one of the great challenges of our time. Implementation of this new approach proposes rethinking the life cycle and every link in the value chain of products and services. It defines seven links: the **design** of the product or service taking into account its environmental impacts throughout the life cycle; **industrial ecology**, which aims to optimise the flow of raw materials and waste through exchanges and sharing between economic operators in the same territory; the **economics of functionality**, that favours use over possession, and tends to sell services related to products rather than the products

52 J. Rifkin, *La troisième révolution industrielle. Comment le pouvoir latéral va transformer l'énergie, l'économie, le monde* (Edition Les liens qui libèrent, 2012). For his system of a circular economy, see the excellent presentation by Anne Rodier in *Le Monde*, 11 December 2012.

themselves, such as the sale of distances rather than tyres; **re-employment**, which returns to the economy goods that no longer meet the needs of the initial consumer, for example the sale of used goods; **repair**, which extends the life of an asset, thereby fighting programmed obsolescence; **re-use**, which saves the maximum number of objects still in running order; and **recycling**, which uses raw materials that can be recovered.

This approach is well suited to the cultural change we are advocating. It redirects strategic decisions towards the public interest. According to Rifkin, it helps reconcile the preservation of natural resources and the dynamism of the economy.

Many companies are beginning to enter this circular economy. Several sectors (automotive, aviation, construction . . .) are launching research and innovating in the very *design* of products to reduce their environmental footprint. Other sectors are introducing the *economy of functionality*. This is particularly the case for Michelin, which began selling distances rather than tyres. This is also the case with car distributors and several other businesses.

Let us pause for a moment and look at an exemplary case of *recycling*, that of **Umicore**, the Belgian rare metals and new materials company. The company has decided to reinvent and transform its core business. From a polluting business of extraction and refining of metals, it has become a world level high-tech enterprise in the field of recovery and treatment of rare metals as well as new materials. It has opted for a culture of sustainable development and raised its game to a high level of performance and profitability. This is what its President and main re-inventor, Thomas Leysen, said:

> Our company has decided to reinvent itself and transform its core business of high pollution mining and extraction to a high-tech, environmentally friendly business. We have adopted a philosophy of sustainable development and, in addition we have excellent financial results . . . Umicore considers sustainable development to be a strategic opportunity and not a constraint. Taking into account, from an early stage in our strategic thinking, the social and environmental impact of our activities offers long-term benefits . . . One thing I am sure of is that this type of development will make the difference between traditional companies and the real 'winners' of tomorrow.

Very close to the previous model are those of the **bio-economy**[53] and **green growth**. This is defined as another type of growth, environmentally friendly growth. It mainly concerns 'green' businesses such as hydro, geothermal and nuclear power, electricity from renewable fuels and waste products, solar and wind. Reports from the ILO (International Labour Organization) and UNEP (UN Environment Programme) show that the transition could affect 1.5 billion jobs worldwide, but in both a positive and negative way. This new type of growth is difficult to quantify, but will in any event be a source of innovation and create jobs. Like any process of creative destruction, however, there will probably also be an economic and social cost. The main argument of environmentalists and some economists is that eventually the cost of inaction will be far greater than action.[54]

3.2.1.3 'Bottom of the pyramid ' and social entrepreneurship

In terms of poverty and inequality, an interesting perspective is that of Amartya Sen. He suggests further focusing the creative ability of the company on

---

53   The set of techniques aimed at using biomass on an industrial scale

54   See in particular, N. Stern, *The Stern Report on Climate Change: The Cost of Inaction* (UK Government, 2006).

the 'bottom of the pyramid':[55] trying, by innovating, to meet the needs of the less creditworthy or non-creditworthy. In focusing on the most disadvantaged, entrepreneurial creativity can help them out of extreme poverty. Trying to awaken their entrepreneurial spirit, it can also awaken a real development dynamic. Some examples are already visible and convincing: the Grameen Bank and microcredit, the Transformational Enterprise Network, Danone Communities, Essilor and Aravind in India, the Shell Foundation, Lafarge South Africa, the Bill & Melinda Gates Foundation . . . Some researchers are working on a new and strong assumption: corporations that voluntarily tackle poverty and fragility, aid the disabled and the marginalised, can themselves be transformed in depth and change their purpose, mind-set and culture.[56]

An interesting example is that of **Essilor**, the world leader in ophthalmic lenses. Its corporate strategy is based on two pillars: scientific and technological leadership and global business leadership. This is a classic approach and has helped the company

55 A. Sen, *Un nouveau modèle économique. Développement, justice, liberté* (Odile Jacob, 2000).
56 Ivan le Mintier, Communication aux Bernardins, 9 October 2010; *Oblat de l'abbaye de Fleury et entrepreneur social*, in Renaissance de Fleury, Avril 2011.

achieve excellent economic and financial perform-ance. In India, Essilor has developed its technological capacity in the service of the poorest. In partnership with an Indian hospital group, Aravind, it takes care of the 'bottom of the pyramid'. For 20 years now, Aravind has provided free cataract operations to the poorest Indians. Essilor has set up laboratories in these field hospitals for eye checks and the manu-facture of lenses. By manufacturing glasses there, it was able to adapt its technology to the cost factor in India's rural market. It is not a question of philan-thropy but of orienting its specific capacity for pro-gress towards the poorest.[57]

Social entrepreneurship has developed in recent years, regardless of commercial enterprises or with their help. It represents a new type of entrepreneur and innovation. This movement tends to place the qualities of the entrepreneur (vision, taste for risk, and ability to convince) in the service of priority social causes.

International organisations have been created to support this new type of entrepreneur and spread their spirit. The most important of them is **Ashoka**,

---

57 This case is described in greater detail in the book by the President of Essilor, Xavier Fontanet: *Et si on faisait confi-ance aux enterprises. L'entreprise française et la mondiali-sation* (Manitoba/Les Belles Lettres, 2010).

founded by Bill Drayton in India in 1980. It aims to support innovative social entrepreneurs in areas such as health, education, training, sustainable development, the fight against discrimination, human rights, etc. It is funded by private funds and entrepreneurs in the business world, and many of its accomplishments are based on the search for complementarities between traditional business and social entrepreneurs. To identify these entrepreneurs, Ashoka uses a philanthropic venture capital approach: careful selection to ensure the novelty of the idea and the entrepreneurial quality of the candidate, financial and professional support for three years, and life-long membership of the Ashoka global network (Ashoka Fellows). This association is present in 70 countries and has helped over 2000 projects.

There are also social venture capital companies aimed at combating poverty through entrepreneurship and promoting local entrepreneurship. This is particularly true of the **Transformational Enterprise Network** founded in the UK by Lord Brian Griffiths and Tim Tan.[58]

Entrepreneurs of this new type are more and more common worldwide. They show that a more social

---

58 B. Griffiths and K. Tan, *Fighting Poverty through Enterprise* (The Transformational Enterprise Network, 2009).

approach to entrepreneurship is not only possible, but can be efficient and sustainable. Innovative initiatives are appearing worldwide and in the most diverse fields. The remarkable book by Darnil and Le Roux[59] shows this in 80 interesting cases in sectors as diverse as sustainable agriculture, bioclimatic architecture, biodiversity, waste management, microfinance, renewable energy . . .

Some responsible companies contribute to the creation and training of local entrepreneurs destined to become a source of development for their region. **Danone** is a great example of this new corporate responsibility, creating a foundation to promote the emergence of young entrepreneurs in the poorest regions: Danone Communities. Its mission is to support and develop local businesses with a sustainable economic model, focused on social goals: to reduce poverty and malnutrition. Alongside social entrepreneurs, this support is provided both by investment through a public mutual fund, but also by technical support through a network of committed experts who lend their experience. The partnership of Danone Communities with the Grameen Bank and Ashoka for social business development centres is an interesting

59 S. Darnil and M. Le Roux, *80 Hommes pour changer le monde. Entreprendre pour la Planète* (JC Lattès, 2005).

extension of this approach. Above and beyond its projects, Danone wants to share its teachings to inspire other individual and collective initiatives in the service of a more cohesive society. This appears to have developed a culture of responsibility in Danone—by focusing its technology and expertise on the 'bottom of the pyramid', it provides an interesting example of responsible entrepreneurship.[60]

3.2.1.4 Economic solidarity and social innovation

Social innovation is defined as any new initiatives—products, services or models—that meet social needs more effectively than existing alternatives, and simultaneously create new social relationships or collaborations.[61] This approach concerns not only the content of innovation but its social implementation. A major theme of this approach is to put people on their feet and make them responsible for their own development. Social innovation not only improves the well-being of society, it strengthens its capacity for initiative and change.

---

60 E. Faber, *Chemins de traverse: vivre l'économie autrement* (Albin Michel, 2012).
61 A. Hubert, *Empowering People, Driving Change: Social Innovation in the European Union*, A Report to the European Commission, July 2010.

This concept is very broad, but the basic idea is close to our own purpose: initiative, inventiveness and creativity are the real sources of change towards progress. Social responsibility is their primary motivation. These innovations give life to a different type of business, with a social rather than profitable purpose, non-dependent on financial markets, and a more participatory approach. They often fill a void or shortcoming in the dynamics of the market economy, although some of them cooperate with capitalist enterprises that can provide technological, managerial or commercial know-how and support. They are leading the way and can serve as an example or even a relay, for the adoption of social responsibility by economic players. These social innovations contribute to the emergence of a new development model, and are probably one of its most powerful drivers. They mobilise enormous energy, talent and capital and are undoubtedly worth more systematic study to increase their effectiveness and fields of action.[62]

Fair trade, which has a long history, is an illustration on a global scale. It has different motivations from those of capitalist enterprises, while being part

62 P. Kourilsky, G. Valentis and N. Caïd, 'The New Initiative of Field Actions Science: FACTS', *FACTS Reports* 2 (2009, http://factsreports.revues.org/228).

of the market. Its purpose is to establish greater justice in competition and trade between the poorest farmers and key players in developed countries. This is achieved by innovation in production and distribution circuits, in the form of funding, in cooperation methods as well as communication with the end consumer, including a certification system, of which Max Havelaar is just one example among others. In their fight against poverty and injustice, Oxfam and World Shops are part of the same approach.

In France, the social economy has developed in many areas. One of the most visible is that of food aid. Restos du coeur and the Epiceries solidaires (solidarity groceries) networks are well-known examples. They are the work of real entrepreneurs and owe their success to important innovations and terms of supply, financing, organisation, cooperation and partnerships. A global solidarity movement, Emmaus Communities were created to fight against causes of poverty by organising mutual aid and relief for the suffering. This NGO was born from an awareness of the social responsibilities of its members to fight injustice. One of its means of action is recovery work that can restore value to any object and increase the opportunities for urgent action to rescue those suffering the most.

More recently, the example, let's call it the arche-type, of social innovation is the Grameen Bank, the village bank, founded by Muhammad Yunus in Bangladesh, and whose model has been extended worldwide. The initial idea was:[63]

> Poverty is very rarely due to personal problems, laziness or a lack of intelligence but always the prohibitive cost of capital, even in very small amounts … What they lack structurally is access to small capital, repayable at fairer rates and over greater time to finance micro-projects … So they can enter the economic loop and generate their own income … a quarter of a century later, the bank is present in 46,000 villages and has already lent over €4.5 billion to twelve million people, 96% of whom are women.

We should also mention the **Bangladesh Rural Advancement Committee** (BRAC), nicknamed the largest NGO in the world. With 130 million beneficiaries, it is managed as a development multinational. Profits are used not to remunerate shareholders but to fund development programmes. This organisation aims to help the poor to become stakeholders in their own development.

---

63 See S. Darnil and M. Le Roux, 2005, op. cit.

3.2.2 Leadership: leaders, architects of creativity and collective consciousness

3.2.2.1 Another type of leader and manager

As we have seen, one of the roles of leaders is to develop the entrepreneurial spirit and creativity of their organisation. Another role is to lead it as a human reality, to motivate its staff and to initiate cultural change for more ethical and sustainable development.

Today, we have enough managers, technicians and financiers. What we lack is a sufficient number of leaders able to design and bring about a change in culture, inspiring those who must implement it and able to create a social legitimacy that is sorely lacking in certain companies.

To do this, we need a new type of leadership.

> Sire, when you look at where good heads have led France, it might be worth trying the bad (Mirabeau to Louis XVI).

The theme of leaders capable of driving a changing society is as old as the world. Societies have 'stalled' mostly because their leaders have failed to adapt and are stuck in thrall to an outdated ideology.

Numerous researches have shown that the most successful companies are those whose leaders manage to establish an adequate balance between their professional skills as managers and their personal leadership qualities.

While Frederick Taylor recommended replacing the government of men with the administration of things, it is almost the opposite that is required today if we want to re-balance the economic, political and ethical dimensions of business.

Giving a narrow definition of *management*, we can say that it mainly concerns the administration of things: goals, budgets, strategic analyses, plans, methods, procedures . . . *Leadership* is the art of driving human reality: it is motivation, communication, participation, the ability to convince people to contribute, as creatively as possible, to the implementation of the strategies and values of the company. The influence of leaders comes from their moral authority. It is through them that ethics become alive in the company.

This in no way detracts from *management* or its methods, the utility and need of which everyone agrees on. When the first man landed on the moon, the director of NASA made a very simple statement: 'The power of the method! This method has allowed ordinary men to do extraordinary things.' Who cannot see in this an approach of considerable power?

As we suggested earlier concerning creativity, should we not put this extraordinary management capacity at the service of major global struggles that we must fight to meet the challenges of climate, poverty and inequality?

Leadership requires more expertise and life skills than merely management techniques. Responsible leadership engages the whole person: mind, heart and spirit. This means deploying all one's intellectual, but also emotional and spiritual, potential.

While man is a being of relationships, the quality and depth of these are always important. Don't we often have to dare to transform a relationship into an encounter?[64] An encounter engages the heart. It is a personalised relationship, on an equal and reciprocal footing, without the mediation of money or power. It is a place of mutual hospitality, listening, caring, the place where one can be 'called by his name', accept one's fragility, recognise others, make them exist, help them stand up. It means rediscovering what it is to be human, to talk to each other, to share ... Communicating means: sharing something in common; con-

---

64 For the whole passage, see J. Vanier, 'Car c'est de l'homme qu'il s'agit', *Rencontres de Nicolas et Dorothée de Flüe* (Saint Maurice, November 2008).

versation means facing each other; dialogue means daring to talk sense.

Should we not dare to give the heart a role in the conduct of organisations? The heart has almost disappeared from our 'systems'. Even in his day, Balzac spoke of 'the polished steel cogs of modern society'. Let us beware of 'the hardening that any form of power produces, the glaciation of the soul'. Let us dare to defy the cynical adage of those who dominate and repeat, giggling with Chamfort: 'man is led with the head; we do not play chess with a good heart'. The responsible leader never sees people as pawns, even if he or she is a financier!

Should we not also dare to speak of consciousness or spirituality? Spirituality does not necessarily mean religion. There is a secular spirituality that might be as vibrant as any religious spirituality. These are the values that guide decisions and behaviour. In an increasingly complex and ambiguous world, this dimension, which is that of consciousness, is essential to the conduct of organisations. Is it not important to recognise this inner force that drives real leaders and allows them to inspire those around them?

3.2.2.2 The responsible leader and ethics

By seeking to be responsible, leaders and companies thus commit themselves to an ethical approach. Responsibility means taking responsibility for one's actions and ensuring their consistency with a value system that is part of a conception of people, society and the future. By acting from a perspective of respect for people and the common good, the business executive becomes an ethical leader. One of his or her responsibilities is to be 'the architect of the collective conscience of the company'.[65]

The new corporate culture involves developing ethics as a core thought that permeates its different levels of action and each of its functions: finance, marketing, research, etc. To achieve this, one may create an **ethical space** in corporations, where this cultural process becomes visible, active and continuous, and is able to face the endless *complexity of reality.*[66] Such a space would be the place where these new attitudes are developed, and where ambiguous matters are questioned and ethical dilemmas discussed, a place of awakening, responding to concerns, a place

---

65 K. Goodpaster, 'The Economy of Gift', *Séminaire Justice et Paix, Rome*, 2011.
66 M. Maesschalk, 'L'éthique entre formalisme et subjectivité', in *L'éthique des affaires* (Louvain la Neuve: Ciaco, 1995).

where the desire to understand other views prevails over the temptation to condemn what is perceived as hostile or simply critical, such as NGOs, for example. A place where we accept questioning, where ethical judgement is developed by comparing what is desirable and what is possible, what causes the greatest good and the least harm, values and realities? A place where a distinction would be made 'between the best and the worst, the extraordinary and the impossible' (Cardinal de Retz). A place where we only accept necessary compromises in full awareness, using our power more lucidly to respond to the challenges and contradictions that beset us. A place that becomes all the more important at ethical moments.

The existence of an ethical space in a company helps workers and leaders find the true freedom they are so often denied by a system that leaves little room for manoeuvre. Such a space would promote communication, transparency, trust, listening and dialogue. It would share the company's difficulties, challenges and the quest for innovative solutions. It would be a place of collective courage to invent and to undertake beyond existing strategies and practices.

3.2.2.3 A staff development policy

Choosing human dignity as a corporate value makes a fundamental difference in relationships, climate, participation, the development of people. It can influence the entire personnel policy of enterprises.

Without responsible leadership at all levels, companies risk not concerning themselves enough about staff, which become a simple 'resource', 'cost', an 'adjustment variable' rather than a valuable investment. This results in alienation, exploitation, disincentives, 'dry' layoffs and the suffering of men and women in the workplace.

Let us remember that many companies implement social policies that emphasise the information, participation and development of their staff. A recent survey in France[67] shows an increase in confidence and satisfaction in areas such as working conditions, career development, organisation and management methods ... The current crisis and increased competitive pressures threaten such an approach but it is essential to keep at it.

People do not work in corporations only as 'homo œconomicus'; they come with all their aspirations: material (to live, have an income, security ...),

---

67 M. Page, Le tableau de bord de la confiance dans l'entreprise, IFOP survey.

symbolic (recognition, power to act, to influence, to be informed . . .) and spiritual (belonging to a meaningful community, sharing experiences, solidarity, fraternity . . .).[68] With increased involvement of their staff in strategy and creativity, transforming them into drivers of progress, corporations would thus exert one of their main social responsibilities. This would also facilitate the emergence of 'intrapreneurs' and a true entrepreneurial culture.

In terms of salaries, it is important to restore a strong link between salaries and productivity. As we have seen above, the disconnect leads to an imbalance between labour income and capital income and a growing sense of injustice. There is an urgent need to redefine the social contract between leaders and employees.

Amartya Sen argues that economic development depends on the development of each person's capacity to promote their real freedoms and enable them to give meaning to their life. Such an approach leads to paying greater attention to what each person is capable of doing and being. It thus makes explicit the contents of a 'life of human dignity'.[69] From the

68 C. Arnsperger, op. cit.
69 M. Nussbaum, op. cit. See also the analysis by Serge Audier in *Le Monde*, 31 August 2012.

perspective of this essay, a key role of leadership is to develop the *creative autonomy* of working people. Should we not strive to ensure their working life is one worth living? Corporations alone cannot succeed in this role, but can make a great contribution, bearing in mind the number of jobs they create.

Wages, working conditions, health and safety are essential, but the key to dignity at work is the degree of *responsibility* that the company gives workers. Even back in 1961, the *Mater et Magistra* encyclical was perfectly clear and strict on this point:

> If the structure and functioning of an economic system are likely to endanger the human dignity of those who work under them, to blunt their sense of responsibility, to remove all their personal initiative, we believe this system to be unjust, even if great riches are produced and are distributed according to the laws of justice and equity.[70]

3.2.3 Statesmanship: executives as citizens, societal dimension and new consultation

A corporation which rediscovers its civic dimension develops its political culture in the full sense of the

---

70 Jean XXIII, *Encyclique Mater et Magistra,* Spes, 1962.

word; it places its actions in the context of the life of the city and participates in discussions on the common good and the direction of our future.

From a policy perspective, corporations become more of a relational entity inserted into institutional and civil society, better meeting their expectations and responding to their questions. Faced with the challenges of the 21st century, responsible leaders engage in societal debates and do not allow one-track thinking to contaminate the planet. By becoming generally more responsible, they help correct the excessive decoupling of economics, politics and ethics. To their role as *entrepreneurs* and *leaders*, should they add that of a citizen engaged in the construction of new governance and adopt, in the English sense of the term, the role of *statesman*? There is therefore a new responsibility which is not only ethical but also political in the societal sense of the term.

Areas of corporate civic responsibility are now beginning to take shape.

Here are some practical topics.

3.2.3.1 Drivers of progress or sowers of doubt?

The implementation of a sustainable development model will not come about by decree. It will only be possible through the 'political' cooperation of all stakeholders. The challenge is great, and all stakeholders need to join forces. Corporations could be a major driver, although many industries have deliberately launched 'doubt strategies' relating to any regulation and any serious transformation of the existing model. They thus pursue a latent struggle to maintain the status quo and defend their sectoral interests. In this area, the power of lobbies is huge and their role should be refocused.

An example of this is the dissemination of doubts about the urgency and nature of measures necessary for the establishment of true sustainable development measures. Proposed by the United Nations, the new model outlines a real plan for the future and aims to deliver economic action in the context of the global common good. At the Earth Summit 1992 in Rio, environmental issues were brought to the top of the international political agenda. The heads of state signed all the texts of the conference, making sustainable development the new priority of UN policies. Since then, despite real progress made by enlightened companies, doubts have been sown by industrial lobbies. Several of them were party to dismantling the concept of sustainable development.

> Their goal was to void it of its disturbing content. They aimed to promote the idea that

> infinite growth is possible in a world with lim-
> ited resource, with no need to question produc-
> tivism as technology will always come to the
> rescue.[71]

Indeed, in 1992, hundreds of scientists, recruited unwittingly, signed the famous Heidelberg Appeal advocating greater distrust of ecological and environmental advocates, accused of pursuing an irrational ideology opposed to scientific and industrial development. It now appears that this call was actually the result of a cleverly orchestrated campaign by a Parisian lobbying firm already closely linked to the asbestos and tobacco industries.[72] So much so that at the International Conference in Rio in 2012, Gro Harlem Brundtland made an alarming call to rescue the Rio negotiations that she deemed almost to be wrecked. Should not the political responsibility of corporations see them engaging their creativity in support of sustainable development rather than in latent resistance to any decisive change?

71 A. Boutaud, *L'empreinte écologique* (La Découverte, 2009); and 'Leurres de la croissance verte', *Le Monde*, 20 June 2012.
72 S. Foucart, 'L'appel d'Heidelberg, une initiative fumeuse', *Le Monde*, 17–18 June 2012. See also *La Fabrique du mensonge* (Denoël, 2013).

In the same vein, other industries have deliberately launched 'doubt strategies' regarding global warming. Their dissemination campaigns of climate-scepticism cast doubt on the scientific consensus that is almost unanimous in this area. According to Naomi Oreskes,[73] climate sceptics and their inspirers are part of a movement that is fighting back against any binding environmental legislation. This movement relies on a society and an era when, thanks to the media, 'everyone can express their opinion, which may well be quoted and repeated, whether true or false, sensible or ridiculous, honest or malicious'. Faced with this 'illusion of democracy', a nuanced, complex and challenging discourse, calling for international cooperation, is necessarily more difficult.[74] In the process, a new discipline has emerged under the name of agnotology.[75] A sort of anti-epistemology, it is the study of how the corporations implement powerful mechanisms aimed at obliteration of knowledge. This powerful conceptual advance is anything but reassuring.

---

73 N. Oreskes and E.M. Conway, *Les marchands de doute* (Editions Le Pommier, 2012).
74 Michel De Muelenaere, 'Des doutes sur le réchauffement du climat', *Le Soir*, 14 March 2011.
75 Editorial, *Le Monde*, 29 October 2011.

The same goes for expertise and the precautionary principle. The most famous case is that of tobacco. Companies in this sector have been convicted of conspiring for 50 years to conceal the dangerous and addictive nature of their products: 'conspiracy to deceive the public about the risk of cancer caused by smoking . . .', 'conduct their business without respect for the truth, the law, the health of the American people . . .', 'organize a public relations campaign to create a false debate on these issues . . .'. In 2004, US prosecutors brought a lawsuit against these companies under the law on corrupt organisations and gangsters.[76]

Public concern generally accompanies new scientific discoveries and major technological changes. We have already talked about the fear caused by poorly explained scientific advances and controversial technological breakthroughs based on expert opinions. It is therefore important to assess the risks objectively and take into account the possible ambiguities of technological progress. In a complex world, it is essential to be able to trust the 'scientific institution'. When there is a definite risk the problem is less difficult because it is merely a case of *prevention*. When the risk is only potential or indeterminable, then it is

76 Racketeer Influenced and Corrupt Organizations Act 1970

precaution and the role of experts is crucial. It is one of the key elements of reasonable conduct. But public authorities or food safety bodies do not always keep pace with scientific advances.

This is where the political responsibility of corporations comes into play. In this area, they should rise to the level of general interest and take an objective approach. But often, thanks to their knowledge of the area they set themselves up as unique experts on the potential risks. They carry out and sometimes sponsor risk assessment commissions. They thus become judge and jury, with a clear conflict of interest. There are still too many cases where sectoral and financial interests prevail over the public interest: drugs, seeds, pesticides, food, financial products . . .

As a result, European society is marked by growing distrust. We have become a safe society tempted by 'zero risk' and the search for scapegoats. Deviations from the precautionary principle are a recent illustration.[77] We see a proliferation of birds of ill omen, prophets of doom and experts in disaster. In such a climate, some major innovations become difficult to implement.

---

77 *L'esprit d'aventure en science et en art,* Colloque de l'Académie Royale de Belgique, 16–18 September 2010.

In a world of rapid scientific progress, increasingly complex and specialised, trusting in 'the experts' becomes more necessary than ever. Only independent experts can inform policymakers and the public. And that is where their status in society is so important. 'Democracy is in danger when the role of the expert is threatened'.[78]

If we want to remain an innovative society, one of creativity and progress, efforts should be made to restore the voice of reason and authority of the intellectual world in informing policy decisions and informing the public. Scientific expertise must play a central role. Its status and procedural forms must be identified and recognised by the public. The ethics of science must be scrupulously respected, including the ethics of communication with the public. Self-proclaimed experts should not have a voice.

A responsible company should redefine its role in this area, working transparently, refraining from being judge and jury and abandoning practices that are unworthy of a corporate citizen.

78 J. Reisse, 'L'expertise scientifique et le choix des experts en question', Académie Royale de Belgique, December 2010. See also: P. de Woot, 'Expertise et société', Académie Royale de Belgique, December 2010.

3.2.3.2 Development of law through the creation of standards

Research by Benoît Frydman[79] shows that the business world is continuously developing rules and standards from which global civil society laws could emerge over time. Technical standards, codes of conduct, labels, all these 'multiple and heterogeneous devices proliferating often anarchically in the most globalised areas' illustrate 'the emergence of global normativity'. Their interest, according to Frydman, is not so much in their formal source or the authority which enacts them, as in 'the important regulating effects they produce'. Global society is not a place of lawlessness, or a large market regulated solely by the law of supply and demand. 'It is a complex and fragmented environment, risky and uncertain, in which stakeholders . . . seek to establish standards that are favourable to their interests'. It is the place of a real 'fight for the right'.

This is where the political dimension of economic players is engaged. The power to set standards and impose them brings with it responsibilities. Standards imposed by corporations cannot result from relationships of strength or the corporate interest

---

79 B. Frydman, 'Comment penser le droit global', in Chérot and Frydman (eds.), *La science du droit dans la globalisation* (Bruxelles: Bruylant, 2012): 17-48.

alone. They must incorporate the ethical and political dimensions discussed in this essay.

The numerous standards which have appeared in the last 20 years often take the form of indicators and labels of social and environmental performance. They aim to increase the transparency of the behaviour of key economic players.

The best known standard is ISO 26000. It aims to help organisations to contribute to sustainable development.[80] It aims to encourage them to go beyond the rule of law, to promote a common understanding in the field of social responsibilities and to complement other instruments and initiatives in this area, not to replace them. It is not intended for certification, regulatory or contractual purposes. This standard was developed by groups emerging from institutions, NGOs, trade unions and businesses of different sizes. The standard defines seven core themes: human rights; conditions and labour relations; the environment; fair operating practices; consumer relations; local communities; and corporate governance.

Another such approach is the United Nations Global Compact. Launched in 2000 by the United Nations at the initiative of Kofi Annan, it is a global pact that commits signatory companies to comply

80 ISO, *Discover ISO 26000*

with a number of values related to the environment, workers' rights, the black economy . . . these companies are required to publish the progress they have made in these areas on an annual basis.

We should also mention the 'ethical codes' that corporations impose on themselves. They may have 'regulatory effects', but these are highly variable. They depend mainly on the corporate culture. If they fail to include ethical and political dimensions, the code will most often be just a matter of public relations. The most striking case is that of Enron, whose code of ethics was awarded the prize for best code in the United States, and whose leaders were jailed a few years later.

There are also a series of indicators that use data published by companies, which contribute to greater visibility of their actions. For this approach, corporate responsibility is limited to the transparency of their behaviour and the accuracy of the information they provide. These steps are a way of emphasising the 'political' dimension of economic action, and may have some influence on companies that deal directly with the public. After a scandal, one official stated that he would now consider a new type of risk: that of public opinion. More positively, it can become a way for companies to build 'soft power' to strengthen their legitimacy and attract the best.

3.2.3.3 A new type of concerted action: the stakeholder's approach

The concept of a 'stakeholder' has been defined by Freeman.[81] It is any group or individual that can affect the objectives of the company or be influenced by them. Stakeholders vary across sectors, but the most common are generally shareholders, the company staff and their unions, suppliers, distributors, the region where the company operates and the public authorities. The influence of stakeholders varies, but they all develop strategies to influence the decisions and behaviour of the company.

The systematic consideration for stakeholders' interests gives the company a 'political' dimension and allows it to integrate other interests or other issues than those of shareholders alone into its decisions. They can thus bring about real change in corporate life. A recent thesis shows that such an approach creates a permanent dialectic process with the various stakeholders.[82] By inserting a constant

---

81 R.E. Freeman, *Strategic Management: A Stakeholder Approach* (Boston, MA: Pitman, 1984).
82 F. Maon, *Toward the stakeholder company. Essay on the role of organizational culture, interaction and change in*

and often confrontational dialogue with stakeholders into the strategic development of corporations, this change provides a more open and dynamic approach to the societal responsibilities of corporations, and can restore their political dimension. It suggests that *statesmanship* is becoming a condition of their long-term success and legitimacy.

This approach advances the debate on corporate social responsibility. It appears as a socially constructed process of strategic decision-making. It also becomes a continuous and plural development process whose purpose goes beyond the interests of shareholders. It reduces the gap between the motivations and influence strategies of different stakeholders. Finally, it shows that these influence strategies are not fixed and may themselves be influenced. Is this not already political?

These ongoing interactions help develop the confidence of stakeholders in the strategies, products and services of the company, thereby reducing the risk of accusations of 'greenwashing' or 'window dressing'. Companies that have adopted this approach consider their social responsibility as value creation: improv-

the pursuit of corporate social responsibility (UCL–Louvain School of Management, 2010).

ing relations with the community, their legitimacy and their business reputation.[83]

This broader consultation is intended to 'clarify and complement traditional governance methods, representative democracy and social negotiation . . . to galvanize them'. It already becomes a reality in the new development models mentioned above, such as the circular economy, the green economy or the social economy.

Partnerships with public authorities are covered by this approach. They are justified when the latter want to keep a guiding and controlling role, with private companies bringing their technological capacity and managerial know-how. For many years, this has been the case for the distribution and purification of municipal water, and this form of action is expanding in the field of new energy. Desertec and major projects in the southern Mediterranean are examples in the field of solar energy. We should also mention projects for large offshore wind farms and the **supergrid** in Europe, and the prospects for renewable marine energy (ocean currents, thermal energy or floating wind farms). Such partnerships are also developing in new areas of urban planning, such as energy efficiency in buildings, urban transport and,

83 Maon and Swaen, op. cit.

more generally, different topics concerning the 'green city' or 'sustainable city'.

3.2.3.4 Increased political participation

The questions raised today by globalisation and techno-science are of major importance for our future. They have no obvious answer. Markets cannot be the only guide to our economic and technological developments—sustainable development concerns all citizens; it is in the public domain. To decide what kind of society we want to create together, should corporations not increase dialogue, listen to other points of view and accept the debate?

Our public men have, besides politics, their private affairs to attend to, and our ordinary citizens, though occupied with the pursuits of industry, are still fair judges of public matters; for, unlike any other nation, regarding him who takes no part in these duties not as unambitious but as useless, we Athenians are able to judge at all events; and, instead of looking on discussion as a stumbling-block in the way of action, we think it an indispensable preliminary to any wise action at all.[84]

---

84 Thucydides, Pericles' discourse on the first casualties of war, in *Histoire de la guerre du Péloponnèse,* trans. J. de Romilly (Paris: Robert Laffont, 1990).

Echoing Pericles, Michel Serres[85] wrote recently:
At the time of the invention of the printing press, Martin Luther said, every man with a bible in his hand is a pope. Now I would say every man with a laptop in hand is a politician. Thanks to the Internet, blogs, Facebook, everyone can speak in a digital commons.

If corporations want to restore the importance of their citizenship, they must develop a political culture in the full sense of the term. They must place their actions within the context of the life of the city, and participate in discussions on the common good and the direction of our future. Beyond mere lobbying, corporate executives and directors should enter into an ongoing dialogue with civil society and governments to contribute to the search for the common good on a worldwide level, as well as the emergence of global governance. This is merely the logical consequence of the broadened *raison d'être* of the business firm and the adoption of the ethics of the future.

Concerning involvement in political debate, are not many leaders still all too often 'useless citizens'? Yet the most enlightened have understood that a cultural change in politics will only come about through

---

85 M. Serres, *Petite Poucette*, Editions du Pommier, 2012; see also his interview in *Le Monde*, 13 April 2012.

acceptance of an open dialogue with those who question our development model.

Several companies are beginning to get involved in the process of civic engagement. The more they do so, the greater influence they will have on the evolution of our business model. But they are obviously not the only ones who need to change. Global regulation is necessary, civil society must continue to invent new forms of solidarity and innovation, and consumers must change their behaviour. This is a collective effort. Moving towards a model of more sustainable and equitable development can only be achieved through a tentative and multifaceted approach.

But without such a commitment, business leaders might remain locked into their instrumental logic and then resemble those of the old regime in France who were incapable of reform.

Of these, many men were able men at their trade; were thoroughly versed in the administrative science of the period; but of the great science of government, the art of watching social movements and foreseeing their results, they were as ignorant as the people themselves; for statesmanship can only be taught by the practical working of free institutions . . . Their minds had stood still at the point where their ancestors had left off . . . Those provincial assemblies which had preserved their old constitution in its integrity were rather a hindrance than a help to civilization. They presented a stolid, impenetrable front to the new spirit of the time.[86]

---

86 A. Tocqueville, from *L'ancien régime et la révolution* (Gallimard, 1952).

For Product Safety Concerns and Information please contact our EU representative GPSR@taylorandfrancis.com Taylor & Francis Verlag GmbH, Kaufingerstraße 24, 80331 München, Germany

Printed and bound by CPI Group (UK) Ltd, Croydon, CR0 4YY
01/05/2025
01858351-0001